The Poetry of Celia Thaxter

Volume II

Celia Laighton Thaxter was born in Portsmouth, New Hampshire on June 29th, 1835 and spent her childhood years on the Isles of Shoals, initially on White Island, where her father, Thomas Laighton, was a lighthouse keeper, and then the wonderfully named Smuttynose and Appledore Islands.

At sixteen, she married Levi Thaxter, her father's business partner, and moved to the mainland, residing first in Watertown, Massachusetts, at a property his father owned. In 1854, they moved to a house in Newburyport and later, in 1856, acquired their own home near the Charles River at Newtonville.

Celia had two sons, one of whom was Roland, born August 28, 1858, and would become a prominent mycologist who would later teach at Harvard.

Her first published poem was written during this time on the mainland. That poem, "Land-Locked", was first published in the Atlantic Monthly in 1861 and earned her $10. It was to be the beginning of a career that would make her one of America's most popular poets and short story writers.

Her marriage with Levi was not perfect, tensions gradually increased. After 10 years she moved back to the islands and her beloved Appledore Island. The marriage was not over but the separations grew longer as Levi didn't share his wife's love of island life.

Celia became the hostess of her father's hotel, the Appledore House, and many New England literary and artists stayed thee; Ralph Waldo Emerson, Nathaniel Hawthorne, Henry Wadsworth Longfellow, Henry David Thoreau, John Greenleaf Whittier, Sarah Orne Jewett, and the artists William Morris Hunt, Childe Hassam, who painted several pictures of her and watercolorist Ellen Robbins, who painted the flowers in her garden.

Celia was present at the time of the infamous murders on Smuttynose Island, about which she wrote the essay, A Memorable Murder which we have included at the end of this volume of poetry.

William Morris Hunt, a close family friend, trying to recover from a debilitating depression, drowned in late summer 1879, an apparent suicide, three days after finishing his last sketch. Celia bore the horror of discovering the body.

That same year, the Thaxters' bought 186 acres on Seapoint Beach on Cutts Island, Kittery Point, where they built a grand Shingle Style "cottage" called Champernowne Farm. In 1880, they auctioned the Newtonville house, and in 1881, moved to their new home.

In March 1888, her friend and fellow poet Whittier hoped "on that lonesome, windy coast where she can only look upon the desolate, winter-bitten pasture-land and the cold grey sea" she could be comforted by "memories of her Italian travels".

Among Celia's most remembered and best loved poems are "The Burgomaster Gull", "Landlocked", "Milking", "The Great White Owl", "The Kingfisher", and "The Sandpiper".

Celia Thaxter died suddenly on August 25th, 1894 on Appledore Island and is buried not far from her cottage, which later burned down in the 1914 fire that consumed The Appledore House hotel.

Index of Contents

Preface
Thora
The Happy Birds
Slumber Song
Starlight
Song: "Hark, how sweet the Thrushes sing!"
Remonstrance
Morning Song
Beethoven
Song: "What good Gift can I bring Thee, thou Dearest"
With the Tide
"The Sunrise never failed us yet"
Enthralled
Song: "Rolls the long Breaker in Splendor, and glances"
Transition
Leviathan
To a Violin
Philosophy
Medrick and Osprey
Alone
Reverie
Heart's-Ease
Autumn
Song: "Love, art Thou weary with the sultry Day?"
Submission
Song: "I wore your Roses, Yesterday"
Spring again
Sonnet: "As happy Dwellers by the Seaside hear"
Song: "Above in her Chamber her Voice I hear"
Foreboding
Homage
Discontent
Already
Guests
Mutation
Farewell
Doubt
Sunset Song
"Love shall save us all"
The Cruise of the Mystery
Schumann's Sonata in A Minor

Because of Thee
Flowers for the Brave
Expostulation
Persistence
S. E
Poor Lisette
To J. G. W
In Tuscany
Good-By, Sweet Day
In Autumn
West-Wind
Impatience
In the Lane
Her Mirror
For Christmas
At Set of Moon
My Garden
Lost and Saved
A Rose of Joy
In September
Under the Eaves
November Morning
In Death's Despite
A Song of Hope
Our Soldiers
Two
Compensation
Sonnet: "Back from Life's Coasts the ebbing Tide had drawn"
Joy
Beloved
The Answer
Song: "Past the Point and by the Beach"
August
Song: "A Bird upon a rosy Bough"
"Oh tell me not of heavenly Halls"
Midsummer
New Year Song
Captured
Faith
At Dawn
In a Horse-Car
A Valentine
Within and Without
Betrothed
Questions
Tyre and Sidon
Hjelma
My Hollyhock

Benediction
Sonnet: "If I do speak your Praise, forgive me, Sweet!"
On the Train
Peace
As Linnets Sing
Ruth
Petition
Appeal

PREFACE

In Volume II of this new edition of the collected writings of Celia Thaxter, great care has been taken to keep to her own arrangement and to the order in which the poems were originally published. In this way they seem to make something like a journal of her daily life and thought, and to mark the constantly increasing power of observation which was so marked a trait in her character. As her eyes grew quicker to see the blooming of flowers and the flight of birds, the turn of the waves as they broke on the rocks of Appledore, so the eyes of her spirit read more and more clearly the inward significance of things, the mysterious sorrows and joys of human life. In the earliest of her poems there is much to be found of that strange insight and anticipation of experience which comes with such gifts of nature and gifts for writing as hers, but as life went on it seemed as if Sorrow were visible to her eyes, a shrouded figure walking in the daylight. Here I and Sorrow sit was often true to the sad vision of her imagination, yet she oftenest came hand in hand with some invisible dancing Joy to a friend's door.

Through the long list of these brief poems (beginning in the earliest book with Land-locked and following through the volumes called Driftweed and The Cruise of the Mystery; all reprinted here with some later verses found together among her papers), one walks side by side in intimate companionship with this sometimes sad-hearted but sincerely glad and happy woman and poet, and knows the springs of her life and the power of her great love and hope. In another volume all her delightful verses and stories for children have been gathered; but one poem, The Sandpiper, seemed to belong to one book as much as to the other, and this has been reprinted in both.

In the volume of her Letters will be found the records of Celia Thaxter's life and so far as it could be told the history of her literary work, while some personal notes by the hand of one of her dearest and oldest friends leave little to be said here. Yet those who have known through her writings alone the islands she loved so much, may care to know how, just before she died, she paid, as if with dim foreboding, a last visit to the old familiar places of the tiny world that was so dear to her. Day after day she called those who were with her to walk or sail; once to spend a long afternoon among the high cliffs of Star Island where we sat in the shade behind the old church, and she spoke of the year that she spent in the Gosport parsonage, and went there with us, to find old memories waiting to surprise her in the worn doorways, and ghosts and fancies of her youth tenanting all the ancient rooms. Once we went to the lighthouse on White Island, where she walked lightly over the rough rocks with wonted feet, and showed us many a trace of her childhood, and sang some quaint old songs, as we sat on the cliff looking seaward, with a touching lovely cadence in her voice, an unforgotten cadence to any one who ever heard her sing. We sat by the Spaniards' graves through a long summer twilight, and she repeated her poem as if its familiar words were new, and we talked of many things as we watched the sea. And on Appledore she showed us all the childish playgrounds dearest to her and to her brothers, — the cupboard in a crevice of rock, the old wells and cellars, the tiny stone-walled enclosures, the worn doorsteps of unremembered houses. We crept under the Sheep rock for shelter out of a sudden gust of rain, we found some of the rarer wild flowers in their secret places. In one of these it thrills me now to remember that she saw a new white flower, strange to her and to the island, which seemed to reach up to her hand. "This never bloomed on Appledore before," she said, and looked at it with grave wonder. "It has not quite bloomed yet," she said, standing before the flower; " I shall come here again; " and then we went our unreturning way up the footpath that led over the ledges, and left the new flower growing in its deep windless hollow on the soft green turf.

It was midsummer, and the bayberry bushes were all a bright and shining green, and we watched a sandpiper, and heard the plaintive cry that begged us not to find and trouble its nest. Under the very rocks and gray ledges, to the far nests of the wild sea birds, her love and knowledge seemed to go. She was made of that very dust, and set about with that sea, islanded indeed in the reserves of her lonely nature with its storms and calmness of high tides, but it seemed as if a little star dust must have been mixed with the ordinary dust of those coasts; there was something bright in her spirit that will forever shine, and light the hearts of those who loved her. It will pass on to a later time in these poems that she wrote of music, of spring and winter, of flowers and birds, and of that northern sea which was her friend and fellow.

S. O. J.

THORA

Come under my cloak, my darling!
Thou little Norwegian maid!
Nor wind, nor rain, nor rolling sea
Shall chill or make thee afraid.

Come close, little blue- eyed maiden,
Nestle within my arm;
Though the lightning leaps and the thunder peals,
We shall be safe from harm.

Swift from the dim horizon
The dark sails scud for the land.
Look, how the rain-cloud drops its fringe
About us on either hand!

And high from our plunging bowsprit
Dashes the cold white spray,
And storm and tumult fill the air
And trouble the summer day.

But thou fearest nothing, darling,
Though the tempest mutter and brood,
Though the wild wind tosses thy bright brown locks,

And flutters thy grass-green snood.

I kiss thy wise white forehead,
While the thunder rolls so grand;
And I hold the curve of thy lovely cheek
In the hollow of my hand;

And I watch the sky and the ocean,
And study thy gentle face —
Its lines of sweetness and power,
The type of thy strong Norse race.

And I wonder what thy life will be,
Thou dear and charming child,
Who hast drifted so far across the world
To a home so lone and wild.

Rude and rough and sad, perhaps;
Anxious, and full of toil;
But I think no sorrow or hardship
Thine inner peace can spoil.

For better than kingly fortunes
Is the wealth that thou dost hold —
A nature perfectly balanced,
A beauty of heart untold.

Thou wilt open the door of patience,
When sorrow shall come and knock;
But to every evil, unworthy thing
Wilt thou the gates fast lock.

So shall thy days be blessed,
Whatever may be thy lot.
But what I am silently pondering
Thou understandest not,

And liftest to me thy steadfast eyes,
Calm as if Heaven looked through.
Do all the maidens in Norway
Have eyes so clear and blue?

See, darling, where, in the distance,
The cloud breaks up in the sky,
And lets a ray of sunshine fall
Where our far-off islands lie!

White they gleam, and the sea grows bright,

And silver shines the foam.
A little space, and our anchor drops
In the haven of Love and Home!

THE HAPPY BIRDS

All about the gable tall swift the swallows flit,
Wheel and call and dart and, fluttering, chatter sweet;
All along the sloping, sunny eaves they perch and sit,
Bright as lapis-lazuli, glittering in the heat.

O spirits of the summer, so dainty, delicate,
Creatures born of sunshine and cheer and all delight,
Pray you, but delay a moment, yet a little wait,
Ere for southern lands again you spread your wings in flight!

Yet the August sun is hot, yet the days are long,
Though the grass is over-ripe and the aster blows;
Still the silence echoes to the sparrow's quiet song,
Still, though late, in thorny thickets lingers the wild rose.

Tarry yet a little, for after you have flown
Lonely all the housetops and still the air will grow;
Where your cheerful voices rang autumn winds will moan;
Presently we shall be dull with winter's weight of snow.

Oh! that we could follow you and cling to Summer's hand,
Ye happy, happy birds, flying lightly through the sky!
Reach with you the rapture of some far, sunny land,
Leave to Winter's bitterness our glad and gay goodby!

SLUMBER SONG

Thou little child, with tender, clinging arms,
Drop thy sweet head, my darling, down and rest
Upon my shoulder, rest with all thy charms;
Be soothed and comforted, be loved and blessed.

Against thy silken, honey-colored hair
I lean a loving cheek, a mute caress;
Close, close I gather thee and kiss thy fair
White eyelids, sleep so softly doth oppress.

Dear little face, that lies in calm content

Within the gracious hollow that God made
In every human shoulder, where He meant
Some tired head for comfort should be laid!

Most like a heavy-folded rose thou art,
In summer air reposing, warm and still.
Dream thy sweet dreams upon my quiet heart;
I watch thy slumber; naught shall do thee ill.

STARLIGHT

The chill, sad evening wind of winter blows
Across the headland, bleak and bare and high,
Rustling the thin, dry grass that sparsely grows,
And shivering whispers like a human sigh.

The sky is thick with stars that sparkle keen,
And great Capella in the clear northeast
Rolls slowly up the cloudless heaven serene,
And the stern uproar of the sea has ceased

A fleeting moment, and the earth seems dead —
So still, so sad, so lonely, and so cold!
Snow- dust beneath me, and above my head
Star-dust in blackness, like thick-sprinkled gold.

The stars of fire, the tiny stars of ice,
The awful whirling worlds in space that wheel,
The dainty crystal's delicate device, —
One hand has fashioned both — and I, who kneel

Here on this winter night, 'twixt stars and snow,
As transient as a snowflake and as weak,
Yearning like all my fellow-men to know
His hidden purpose that no voice may speak;

In silent awe I watch his worlds: I see
Mighty Capella' s signal, and I know
The steady beam of light that reaches me
Left the great orb full seventy years ago.

A human lifetime! Reason strives in vain
To grasp at time and space, and evermore
Thought, weary grown and baffled, must again
Retrace its slow steps to the humble door

Of wistful patience, there to watch and wait
Devoutly, till at last Death's certain hand,
Imperious, opens wide the mystic gate
Between us and the future He has planned.

Yea, Death alone. But shall Death conquer all?
Love fights and pleads in anguish of despair.
Sooner shall great Capella wavering fall
Than any voice respond to his wild prayer.

And yet, what fire divine makes hope to glow
Through the pale ashes of our earthly fate?
Immortal hope, above all joy, below
All depths of pain wherein we strive and wait!

Dull is our sense; hearing we do not hear,
And seeing see not; yet we vaguely feel
Somewhere is comfort in the darkness drear,
And, hushing doubts and fears, we learn to kneel.

Starlight and silence! Dumb are sky and sea;
Silent as death the awful spaces lie;
Speechless the bitter wind blows over me,
Sad as the breathing of a human sigh.

SONG

Hark, how sweet the thrushes sing!
Hark, how clear the robins call!
Chorus of the happy spring,
Summer's madrigal!

Flood the world with joy and cheer,
O ye birds, and pour your song
Till the farthest distance hear
Notes so glad and strong!

Storm the earth with odors sweet,
O ye flowers, that blaze in light!
Crowd about June's shining feet,
All ye blossoms bright.

Shout, ye waters, to the sun!

Back are winter's fetters hurled;

Summer's glory is begun;
Beauty holds the world!

REMONSTRANCE

"Come out and hear the birds sing! Oh, wherefore sit you there
At the western window watching, dreamy-pale and still and fair,
While the warm summer wind disparts your tresses' clustering gold?
What is it on the dim sea line your eyes would fain behold?"
"I seek a sail that never looms from out the purple haze
At rosy dawn, or fading eve, or in the noontide's blaze.

"A sail? Lo, many a column of white canvas far and near!
All day they glide across the blue, appear and disappear;
See, how they crowd the offing, flocking from the sultry South!
Why stirs a smile more sad than tears the patience of your mouth? "
"They lean before the freshening breeze, they cross the ocean floor,
But the ship that brings me tidings of my love comes never more."

"Come out into the garden where the crimson phloxes burn,
And every slender lily-stem upbears a lustrous urn;
A thousand greetings float to you from bud and bell and star,
Their sweetness freights the breathing wind; how beautiful they are!"
"Their brilliant color blinds me; I sicken at their breath;
The whisper of this mournful wind is sad to me as death."

"And must you sit so white and cold while all the world is bright?
Ah, come with me and see how all is brimming with delight!
On the beach the emerald breaker murmurs o'er the tawny sand;
The white spray from the rock is tossed, by melting rainbows spanned."
"Nay, mock me not! I have no heart for nature's happiness;
One sound alone my soul can fill, one shape my sight can bless."

"And are your fetters forged so fast, though you were free and strong,
By the old, mysterious madness, told in story and in song
Since burdened with the human race the world began to roll?
Can you not thrust the weight away, so heavy on your soul?"
"There is no power in earth or heaven such madness to destroy,
And I would not part with sorrow that is sweeter far than joy."

"Oh marvelous content, that from such still despair is born!
Nay, I would wrestle with my fate till love were slain with scorn!
O mournful Mariana! I would never sit so pale,
Watching, with eyes grown dim with dreams, the coming of a sail! "
"Peace, peace! How can you measure a depth you never knew?
My chains to me are dearer than your freedom is to you.

MORNING SONG

We launch our boat upon the sparkling sea,
We dip our rhythmic oars with song and cheer;
Before our dancing prow the shadows flee,
Behind us fast the fair coasts disappear.

So fade our childhood's shores. Without regret
We leave the safe, green, happy fields, and try
The vague, uncertain ocean, storm-beset,
Nor see the tempests that before us lie.

Mushed with our hope the unknown future gleams,
Freighted with blissful dreams our barque floats on,
And life a shining path of victory seems,
Crowned with a golden peace when day is done.

BEETHOVEN

If God speaks anywhere, in any voice,
To us, his creatures, surely here and now
We hear Him, while the great chords seem to bow
Our heads, and all the symphony's breathless noise
Breaks over us with challenge to our souls!
Beethoven's music! From the mountain peaks
The strong, divine, compelling thunder rolls,
And, " Come up higher, come! " the words it speaks,
"Out of your darkened valleys of despair,
Behold, I lift you upon mighty wings
Into Hope's living, reconciling air!
Breathe, and forget your life's perpetual stings;
Dream, — folded on the breast of Patience sweet,
Some pulse of pitying love for you may beat!"

SONG

What good gift can I bring thee, thou dearest!
All joys to thee belong;
Thy; praise from loving lips all day thou nearest,
Sweeter than any song.

For thee the sun shines and the earth rejoices
In fragrance, music, light;
The spring-time woos thee with a thousand voices,
For thee her flowers are bright;

Youth crowns thee, and love waits upon thy splendor,
Trembling beneath thine eyes;
The morning sky is yet serene and tender,
Thy life before thee lies.

What shall I bring thee, thou dearest, fairest!
Thou holdest in thy hand
My heart as lightly as the rose thou wearest;
Nor wilt thou understand

Thou art my sun, my rose, my day, my morrow,
My lady proud and sweet!
I bring the treasure of a priceless sorrow,
To lay before thy feet.

WITH THE TIDE

Swift o'er the water my light yacht dances,
Flying fast from the wind of the South;
Bright from her bowsprit the white foam glances,
And straight we steer for the harbor's mouth.

The coast line dim from the haze emerges,
With tender tints of the spring-time toned;
On silver beaches roll sparkling surges,
And woods are green on the hills enthroned.

The sentinel lighthouses watch together,
As the stately river we reach at last;
The robins sing in the blithe May weather,
And the flood-tide bears us onward fast.

From bank to bank flows a chorus mellow
Of rippling frogs and of singing birds;
The fields are starry with flowers of yellow,
And green slopes pasture the lowing herds.

A lovely perfume blows softly over
From apple-blossoms on either side,
From golden willow and budding clover,
And many a garden of lowly pride.

And a lazy echo of glad cocks crowing
From door-yards cosy rings far and near!
And the city's murmur is slowly growing
From out the distance distinct and clear.

Over the river, so broadly flowing,
Cottages look from the sheltering trees;
And out through the orchard, with blossoms snowing,
Comes a brown-haired maiden from one of these.

She waves her hand as in friendly token,
And watches my swift boat sailing on;
I answer her signal — no word is spoken,
'T is but a moment, and she is gone.

And when, from the far-off town returning,
Dropping down with the ebbing tide,
Seaward we sail, with the sunset burning
O'er wastes of the ocean, lone and wide,

Again in the orchard her white hand lifted
Shows like a waft of a sea-bird's wing,
While the rosy blossoms are o'er her drifted,
And loud with rapture the robins sing.

I know her not and shall know her never,
But ever I watch for that friendly sign;
And up or down with the stately river
Her lovely greeting is always mine.

And her presence lends to the scene a glory,
More beauty to blossom and stream and tree;
And back o'er the wastes of the ocean hoary
Her gentle image I take with me.

"THE SUNRISE NEVER FAILED US YET"

Upon the sadness of the sea
The sunset broods regretfully;
From the far lonely spaces, slow
Withdraws the wistful afterglow.

So out of life the splendor dies;
So darken all the happy skies;
So gathers twilight, cold and stern;

But overhead the planets burn;

And up the east another day
Shall chase the bitter dark away;
What though our eyes with tears be wet
The sunrise never failed us yet.

The blush of dawn may yet restore
Our light and hope and joy once more.
Sad soul, take comfort, nor forget
That sunrise never failed us yet!

ENTHRALLED

Like huge waves, petrified, against the sky,
The solemn hills are heaved; by shadow kissed,
Or softly touched by delicate light they lie
Melting in sapphire and in amethyst.

The thronging mountains, crowding all the scene,
Are like the long swell of an angry sea,
Tremendous surging tumult that has been
Smitten to awful silence suddenly.

The nearer slopes with autumn glory blaze,
Garnet and ruby, topaz, amber, gold;
Up through the quiet air the thin smoke strays
From many a lonely homestead, brown and old.

The scattered cattle graze in pastures bare,
The brooks sing unconcerned beside the way,
Belated crickets chirp, while still and fair
Dies into sunset peace the golden day.

And toward the valley, where the little town
Beckons with twinkling lights, that gleam below
Like bright and friendly eyes, we loiter down
And find our shelter and our fireside glow.

But while the gay hours pass with laugh and jest,
And all is radiant warmth and joy once more,
My captured thought must wander out in quest
Of that vast mountain picture, o'er and o'er;

Where underneath the black and star-sown arch
Earth's ancient trouble speaks eternally;

And I must watch those mighty outlines march
In silence, motionless, with none to see;

While from the north the night- wind sighing sweeps,
And, sharp against the crystal sky relieved,
The tumult of forgotten ages sleeps
Where like huge waves the solemn hills are heaved.

SONG

Rolls the long breaker in splendor, and glances,
Leaping in light!
Sparkling and singing the swift ripple dances,
Laughing and bright;
Up through the heaven the curlew is flying,
Soaring so high!
Sweetly lils wild notes are ringing, and dying,
Lost in the sky.
Glitter the sails to the south-wind careening,
White-winged and brave;
Bowing to breeze and to billow, and leaning
Low o'er the wave.
Beautiful wind, with the touch of a lover
Leading the hours,
Helping the winter-worn world to recover
All its lost flowers,
Gladly I hear thy warm whisper of rapture,
Sorrow is o'er!
Earth all her music and bloom shall recapture,
Happy once more.

TRANSITION

A clash of human tongues within
Made the bright room a dreary jail;
Dull webs of talk the idle spin
Turned all its glow and color pale.

Outside, the peaceful sunset sky
Was burning, deepening with the night;
One great star, glittering still and high,
Sent o'er the sea its track of light.

And wearily I spoke, and heard

An empty echo of reply,
Fretting like some imprisoned bird
That longs to break its cage and fly;

When suddenly the din seemed stilled,
Rarer the air so dense before;
A mystic rapture warmed and thrilled
My heart, and I was dull no more.

Joy stole to me with sweet surmise,
With sense of some unmeasured good;
There was no need to lift my eyes
To know who on the threshold stood,

More splendid than the brilliant night
That looked in at the window-pane,
Welcome as to parched fields the light,
Refreshing touch of summer rain!

She moved with recognition sweet,
She bowed with courtesy calm and kind,
As graceful as the waving wheat
That bends before the summer wind.

Swift sped the step of lagging time,
As if a breeze of morning blew;
Clear as the ring of Chaucer's rhyme
The vapid, idle talking grew!

I heard her rich tones sounding through
The many voices like a strain
Of lofty music, strong and true,
And perfect joy was mine again.

I did not seek her radiant face,
Bright as spring light when winter dies,
But warm across the crowded space
I felt the gaze of noble eyes;

And in that glorious look, at last,
I seemed like one with sins forgiven,
With all life's pain and sorrow passed,
Entering the open gates of heaven!

LEVIATHAN

Betwixt the bleak rock and the barren shore
Rolled miles of hoary waves that hissed with frost,
And from the bitter north with sullen roar
Swept the wild wind, and the wild water tossed.

In the cold sky, hard, pitiless, and drear,
The sun dropped down; but ere the world grew gray,
A sweet, reluctant rose-tint, sad and clear,
Stained icy crags and leagues of leaping spray.

Midway between the lone rock and the shore
A fountain fair sprang skyward suddenly,
And sudden fell, and yet again once more
The column rose, and sank into the sea.

Silent, ethereal, mystic, delicate,
Flushed with delicious glow of fading rose,
It grew and vanished, like some genie great,
Some wild, thin phantom, woven of winter snows.

'T was the foam-fountain of the mighty whale,
Rising each time more far and faint and dim.
All his huge strength against the thundering gale
He set; no hurricane could hinder him!

There came to me a gladness in the sight,
A pleasure in the thought of life so strong,
Daring the elements, and making light
Of winter's wrathful power of wreck and wrong.

I gloried in his triumph o'er the vast
Blind rage of Nature. All her awful force,
The terror of her tempest full she cast
Against him, yet he kept his ponderous course.

For her worst fury he nor stayed nor turned.
'T was joy to think in such tremendous play,
Through the sea's cruelty, all unconcerned,
Leviathan pursued his placid way!

TO A VIOLIN

What wondrous power from heaven upon thee wrought?
What prisoned Ariel within thee "broods?
Marvel of human skill and human thought,
Light as a dry leaf in the winter woods!

Thou mystic thing, all beautiful! What mind
Conceived thee, what intelligence began
And out of chaos thy rare shape designed,
Thou delicate and perfect work of man?

Across my hands thou liest mute and still;
Thou wilt not breathe to me thy secret fine;
Thy matchless tones the eager air shall thrill
To no entreaty or command of mine;

But comes thy master, lo! thou yieldest all:
Passion and pathos, rapture and despair;
To the soul's need thy searching voice doth call
In language exquisite beyond compare,

Till into speech articulate at last
Thou seem'st to break, and thy charmed listener hears
Thee waking echoes of the vanished past,
Touching the source of gladness and of tears;

And with bowed head he lets the sweet wave roll
Across him, swayed by that weird power of thine,
And reverence and wonder fill his soul
That man's creation should be so divine.

PHILOSOPHY

So soon the end must come,
Why waste in sighs our breath?
So soon our lips are dumb,
So swift comes death.

So brief the time to smile,
Why darken we the air
With frowns and tears, the while
We nurse despair?

Hold firm the suffering will
And bravely thrust it back;
Fight with the powers of ill,
The legions black.

Stand in the sunshine sweet
And treasure every ray,
Nor seek with stubborn feet

The darksome way.

Have courage! Keep good cheer!
Our longest time is brief.
To those who hold you dear
Bring no more grief.

But cherish blisses small,
Grateful for least delight
That to your lot doth fall,
However slight.

And lo! all hearts will bring
Love, to make glad your days:
Blessings untold will spring
About your ways.

So shall life bloom and shine,
Lifted its pain above,
Crowned with this gift divine,
The gift of Love.

MEDRICK AND OSPKEY

Medrick, waving wide wings low over the breeze- rippled bight;
Osprey, soaring superb overhead in the fathomless blue,
Graceful and fearless and strong, do you thrill with the morning's delight
Even as I? Brings the sunshine a message of beauty for you?

Oh the blithe breeze of the west, blowing sweet from the far-away land,
Bowing the grass heavy-headed, thick crowding, so slender and proud!
Oh the warm sea sparkling over with waves by the swift wind fanned!
Oh the wide sky crystal clear, with bright islands of delicate cloud!

Feel you the waking of life in the world locked long time in the frost,
Beautiful birds, with the light flashing bright from your banner-like wings?
Osprey, soaring on high, in the depths of the sky half lost,
Medrick, hovering low where the sandpiper's sweet note rings!

Nothing am I to you, a blot, perhaps, on the day;
Naught do I add to your joy, but precious you are in my sight;
And you seem on your glad wings to lift me up into the ether away,
And the morning divine is more radiant because of your glorious flight.

ALONE

The lilies clustered fair and tall;
I stood outside the garden wall;
I saw her light robe glimmering through
The fragrant evening's dusk and dew.

She stooped above the lilies pale;
Up the clear east the moon did sail;
I saw her bend her lovely head
O'er her rich roses blushing red.

Her slender hand the flowers caressed,
Her touch the unconscious blossoms blessed;
The rose against her perfumed palm
Leaned its soft cheek in blissful calm.

I would have given my soul to be
That rose she touched so tenderly!
I stood alone, outside the gate,
And knew that life was desolate.

REVERIE

The white reflection of the sloop's great sail
Sleeps trembling on the tide;
In scarlet trim her crew lean o'er the rail,
Lounging on either side.

Pale blue and streaked with pearl the waters lie
And glitter in the heat;
The distance gathers purple bloom where sky
And glimmering coast-line meet.

From the cove's curving rim of sandy gray
The ebbing tide has drained,
Where, mournful, in the dusk of yesterday
The curlew's voice complained.

Half lost in hot mirage the sails afar
Lie dreaming, still and white;
No wave breaks, no wind breathes, the peace to mar;
Summer is at its height.

How many thousand summers thus have shone
Across the ocean waste,

Passing in swift succession, one by one,
By the fierce winter chased!

The gray rocks blushing soft at dawn and eve,
The green leaves at their feet,
The dreaming sails, the crying birds that grieve,
Ever themselves repeat.

And yet how dear and how forever fair
Is Nature's friendly face,
And how forever new and sweet and rare
Each old familiar grace!

What matters it that she will sing and smile
When we are dead and still?
Let us be happy in her beauty while
Our hearts have power to thrill.

Let us rejoice in every moment bright,
Grateful that it is ours;
Bask in her smiles with ever fresh delight,
And gather all her flowers;

For presently we part: what will avail
Her rosy fires of dawn,
Her noontide pomps, to us, who fade and fail,
Our hands from hers withdrawn!

HEART'S-EASE

Southward still the sun is slanting day by day,
Skies that brim with gold and azure slowly change;
Beauty waxes cold and dim and cannot stay,
Into tone and tint steals something ill and strange.

Threat of evil finds its way to every ear,
Lurks in light and shade and sounds in every breath;
From the pathless snow-fields comes a warning drear,
And the shuddering north-wind carries news of g, death.

Stealthy step of Winter near and nearer draws:
Locking earth beneath him, terrible with might,
Strides he from the icy zone without a pause,
Swift and sure and fierce, with ready hand to smite.

Dearest, when without the door he threatening stands,

Having rendered desolate the fair green earth,
And sent her happy birds to sunnier lands,
And choked with sullen snows her summer mirth,

We shall sit together, you and I, once more,
Warm and quiet, shut away from storm and cold;
We shall smile to hear him blustering at the door,
While the room glows with the firelight's ruddy gold.

How safe my heart keeps every memory sweet,
Holding still your picture, as you used to sit,
Ever lovely, full of grace from head to feet,
With that heap of snowy wool I watched you knit;

With the lamplight falling on your cloudy hair —
On the rich, loose bands of brown, so soft to touch;
On the silken knot of rose you used to wear,
On the thoughtful little face I love so much.

You remember, when aloud I read to you,
Sometimes silence intervened. You would not move,
But in your radiant cheek the blushes grew,
For you knew I paused to gaze at you, my love!

Paused to realize my heaven, till with kind,
Clear and questioning gray eyes you sought my face
What a look! Its kindling glory struck me blind;
'T was a splendor that illumined all the place.

What to us are Winter's blows and hate and wrath?
And what matter that the green earth's bloom is fled?
There has been immortal summer in our path
All the happy, happy years since we were wed.

AUTUMN

Round and round the garden rushed a sudden blast,
Crying, "Autumn! Autumn!" shuddering as it passed.
Dry poppy-head and larkspur- spike shrill whistled in the wind,
Together whispering, "Autumn! and Winter is behind!"

Tossed the sumach pennons, green and gold and red;
Flapped the awning scallops loudly overhead;
Swung the empty hammocks lightly to and fro;
While the crickets simmered, chirruping below.

Keen the star of evening hung glittering in the sky,
Red the west was burning, deepening silently;
Summer constellations slow wheeling out of sight,
Great Orion shining clear upon the face of night.

Sadly sang the ocean, sighing in the dark;
Far away the lighthouse lit a sudden spark;
Black against the sunset sails were gliding past;
Earth and sea and sky were saying, "Autumn 's here at last!"

Soon will snow be flying, soon will tempests roar,
Soon the freezing north will lash us bitter as before;
I heard the waters whisper, I heard the winds complain,
But sweet, reluctant Summer I knew would come again.

SONG

Love, art thou weary with the sultry day?
Fain would I be the cool and delicate air
About the whiteness of thy brow to play,
And softly, lightly stir thy cloudy hair.

Upon thy head doth the fierce winter smite,
And shudderest thou in darkness cold to be?
I would I were the coming of the light,
Shelter, and radiant warmth to comfort thee.

I would be fire and fragrance, light and air,
All gracious things that serve thee at thy need;
Music, to lift thy heart above all care;
The wise and charming book that thou dost read.

There is no power that cheers and blesses thee
But I do envy it, beneath the sun!
Thy health, thy rest, thy refuge I would be;
Thy heaven on earth, thine every good in one.

SUBMISSION

The sparrow sits and sings, and sings;
Softly the sunset's lingering light
Lies rosy over rock and turf,
And reddens where the restless surf
Tosses on high its plumes of white.

Gently and clear the sparrow sings,
While twilight steals across the sea,
And still and bright the evening-star
Twinkles above the golden bar
That in the west lies quietly.

Oh, steadfastly the sparrow sings,
And sweet the sound; and sweet the touch
Of wooing winds; and sweet the sight
Of happy Nature's deep delight
In her fair spring, desired so much!

But while so clear the sparrow sings
The crashing of the riven wreck,
Breakers that sweep the shuddering deck,
And sounds of agony and fear.

How is it that the birds can sing?
Life is so full of bitter pain;
Hearts are so wrung with hopeless grief;
Woe is so long and joy so brief;
Nor shall the lost return again.

Though rapturously the sparrow sings,
No bliss of Nature can restore
The friends whose hands I clasped so warm,
Sweet souls that through the night and storm
Fled from the earth for evermore.

Yet still the sparrow sits and sings,
Till longing, mourning, sorrowing love,
Groping to find what hope may be
Within death's awful mystery,
Reaches its empty arms above;

And listening, while the sparrow sings,
And soft the evening shadows fall,
Sees, through the crowding tears that blind,
A little light, and seems to find
And clasp God's hand, who wrought it all.

SONG

I wore your roses yesterday:
About this light robe's folds of white,

Wherein their gathered sweetness lay,
Still clings their perfume of delight.

And all in vain the warm wind sweeps
These airy folds like vapor fine,
Among them still the odor sleeps,
And haunts me with a dream divine.

So to my heart your memory clings,
So sweet, so rich, so delicate:
Eternal summer-time it brings,
Defying all the storms of fate;

A power to turn the darkness bright,
Till life with matchless beauty glows;
Each moment touched with tender light,
And every thought of you a rose!

I stood on the height in the stillness
And the planet's outline scanned,
And half was drawn with the line of sea
And half with the far blue land.

SPRING AGAIN

With wings that caught the sunshine
In the crystal deeps of the sky,
Like shapes of dreams, the gleaming gulls
Went slowly floating by.

Below me the boats in the harbor
Lay still, with their white sails furled
Sighing away into silence,
The breeze died off the world.

On the weather-worn, ancient ledges
Peaceful the calm light slept;
And the chilly shadows, lengthening,
Slow to the eastward crept.

The snow still lay in the hollows,
And where the salt waves met
The iron rock, all ghastly white
The thick ice glimmered yet.

But the smile of the sun was kinder,

The touch of the air was sweet;
The pulse of the cruel ocean seemed
Like a human heart to beat.

Frost-locked, storm-beaten, and lonely,
In the midst of the wintry main,
Our bleak rock yet the tidings heard:
"There shall be spring again! "

Worth all the waiting and watching,
The woe that the winter wrought,
Was the passion of gratitude that shook
My soul at the blissful thought!

Soft rain and flowers and sunshine,
Sweet winds and brooding skies,
Quick-flitting birds to fill the air
With clear, delicious cries;

And the warm sea's mellow murmur
Resounding day and night;
A thousand shapes and tints and tones
Of manifold delight,

Nearer and ever nearer
Drawing with every day!
But a little longer to wait and watch
'Neath skies so cold and gray,

And hushed is the roar of the bitter north
Before the might of the Spring,
And up the frozen slope of the world
Climbs Summer, triumphing.

SONNET

As happy dwellers by the seaside hear
In every pause the sea's mysterious sound,
The infinite murmur, solemn and profound,
Incessant, filling all the atmosphere,
Even so I hear you, for you do surround
My newly- waking life, and break for aye
About the viewless shores, till they resound
With echoes of God's greatness night and day.
Refreshed and glad I feel the full flood-tide
Fill every inlet of my waiting soul;

Long-striving, eager hope, beyond control,
For help and strength at last is satisfied;
And you exalt me, like the sounding sea,
With ceaseless whispers of eternity.

SONG

Above in her chamber her voice I hear
Singing so clear;
Among her flowers I stand and wait,
Dreaming I lean on the garden gate,
In joy and fear.

Softly the light robes she doth wear
Sweep down the stair;
O eager heart, less wildly beat, —
I shall behold her, stately, sweet,
All good and fair!

Nearer, her voice! In a moment more
Through the open door
Come grace and beauty and all delight
The round world holds to my dazzled sight,
The threshold o'er!

She holds me mute with her beaming eyes
Full of bright surprise;
Still grow the pulses her coming shook,
In the gentle might of her golden look
My heaven lies!

FOREBODING

Cricket, why wilt thou crush me with thy cry?
How can such light sound weigh so heavily!
Behold the grass is sere, the cold dews fall,
The world grows empty — yes, I know it all,
The knell of joy I hear.

Oh, long ago the swallows hence have flown,
And sadly sings the sea in undertone;
The wild vine crimsons o'er the rough gray stone;
The stars of winter rise, the cool winds moan;
Fast wanes the golden year.

O cricket, cease thy sorrowful refrain
This summer's glory comes not back again,
But others wait with flowers and sun and rain;
Why wakest thou this haunting sense of pain,
Of loss, regret, and fear?

Clear sounds thy note above the waves' low sigh,
Clear through the breathing wind that wanders by,
Clear through the rustle of dry grasses tall;
Thou chantest, "Joy is dead!" I know it all,
The winter's woe is near.

HOMAGE

Nay, comrade, 't is a weary path we tread
Through this world's desert spaces, dull and dry,
And long ago died out youth's morning-red,
And low the sunset fires before us lie:

And you are worn, though brave the face you wear.
Forbear the deprecating gesture, take
The honest admiration that I bear
Your genius, and be mute, for friendship's sake

Up to your lips I lift a generous wine,
Pure, perfumed, potent, living, sparkling bright;
A deep cup, brimming with a draught divine;
Drink, then, and be refreshed with my delight.

It gladdens you? You know the gift sincere?
You dreamed not life yet held a thing so sweet?
Nay, noble friend, your thanks I will not hear,
But I shall cast my roses at your feet,

And go my way rejoicing that 't is I
Who recognize, acknowledge, judge you best,
Proud that a star so steadfast lights the sky,
And in the power of blessing you most blest.

DISCONTENT

There is no day so dark
But through the murk some ray of hope may steal.

Some blessed touch from Heaven that we might feel,
If we but chose to mark.

We shut the portals fast,
And turn the key and let no sunshine in;
Yet to the worst despair that comes through sin
God's light shall reach at last.

We slight our daily joy,
Make much of our vexations, thickly set
Our path with thorns of discontent, and fret
At our fine gold's alloy,

Till bounteous Heaven might frown
At such ingratitude, and, turning, lay
On our impatience burdens that would weigh
Our aching shoulders down.

We shed too many tears,
And sigh too sore, and yield us up to woe,
As if God had not planned the way we go
And counted out our years.

Can we not be content,
And lift our foreheads from the ignoble dust
Of these complaining lives, and wait with trust,
Fulfilling Heaven's intent?

Must we have wealth and power,
Fame, beauty, all things ordered to our mind
Nay, all these things leave happiness behind!
Accept the sun and shower,

The humble joys that bless,
Appealing to indifferent hearts and cold
"With delicate touch, striving to reach and hold
Our hidden consciousness;

And see how everywhere
Love comforts, strengthens, helps, and saves us all;
What opportunities of good befall
To make life sweet and fair!

ALREADY

Already the dandelions

Are changed into vanishing ghosts;
Already the tall ripe grasses
Are standing in serried hosts,

Bowing with stately gesture
Whenever the warm winds blow,
Like the spear-heads of an army
Charging against the foe.

Already the nestling sparrows
Are clothed in a mist of gray,
And under the breast of the swallow
The warm eggs stir to-day.

Already the cricket is busy
With hints of soberer days,
And the goldenrod lights slowly
Its torch for the autumn blaze.

O brief, bright smile of summer!
O days divine and dear!
The voices of winter's sorrow
Already we can hear.

And we know that the frosts will find us,
And the smiling skies grow rude,
While we look in the face of Beauty,
And worship her every mood.

GUESTS

Sunflower tall and hollyhock, that wave in the wind together,
Cornflower, poppy, and marigold, blossoming fair and fine,
Delicate sweet- peas, glowing bright in the quiet autumn weather,
While over the fence, on fire with bloom, climbs the nasturtium vine!

Quaint little wilderness of flowers, straggling hither and thither —
Morning-glories tangled about the larkspur gone to seed,
Scarlet runners that burst all bounds, and wander, heaven knows whither,
And lilac spikes of bergamot, as thick as any weed.

And oh, the bees and the butterflies, the humming-birds and sparrows,
That over the garden waver and chirp and flutter the livelong day!
Humming-birds, that dart in the sun like green and golden arrows,
Butterflies like loosened flowers blown off by the wind in play.

Look at the red nasturtium flower, drooping, bending, and swaying;
Out the gold-banded humble-bee breaks and goes booming anew!
Hark, what the sweet-voiced fledgeling sparrows low to themselves are saying,
Pecking my golden oats where the cornflowers gleam so blue!

Welcome, a thousand times welcome, ye dear and delicate neighbors —
Bird and bee and butterfly, and humming-bird fairy fine!
Proud am I to offer you a field for your graceful labors;
All the honey and all the seeds are yours in this garden of mine.

I sit on the doorstep and watch you. Beyond lies the infinite ocean,
Sparkling, shimmering, whispering, rocking itself to rest;
And the world is full of perfume and color and beautiful motion,
And each new hour of this sweet day the happiest seems and best.

MUTATION

About your window's happy height
The roses wove their airy screen:
More radiant than the blossoms bright
Looked your fair face between.

The glowing summer sunshine laid
Its touch on field and flower and tree;
But 'twas your golden smile that made
The warmth that gladdened me.

The summer withered from the land,
The vision from the window passed:
Blank Sorrow looked at me; her hand
Sought mine and clasped it fast.

The bitter wind blows keen and drear,
Stinging with winter's flouts and scorns,
And where the roses breathed I hear
The rattling of the thorns.

FAREWELL

The crimson sunset faded into gray;
Upon the murmurous sea the twilight fell;
The last warm breath of the delicious day
Passed with a mute farewell.

Above my head, in the soft purple sky,
A wild note sounded like a shrill-voiced bell;
Three gulls met, wheeled, and parted with a cry
That seemed to say, "Farewell!"

I watched them: one sailed east, and one soared west,
And one went floating south; while like a knell
That mournful cry the empty sky possessed,
"Farewell, farewell, farewell!"

"Farewell!" I thought, it is the earth's one speech;
All human voices the sad chorus swell;
Though mighty Love to heaven's high gate may reach,
Yet must he say, "Farewell!"

The rolling world is girdled with the sound,
Perpetually breathed from all who dwell
Upon its bosom, for no place is found
Where is not heard, "Farewell!"

"Farewell, farewell!" — from wave to wave 'tis tossed,
From wind to wind: earth has one tale to tell;
All other sounds are dulled and drowned and lost
In this one cry, "Farewell!"

DOUBT

The wild rose blooms for the sun of June,
The tide ebbs slowly out;
I hear in the dreamy afternoon
The far-off fisher's shout.

The sand lies gray and the sea leaps blue,
The tide ebbs slowly out;
lover mine, who called to you,
That you left me here to doubt?

The white gull's wing sweeps the whiter foam,
The tide ebbs slowly out;
'T is not your white sail, yearning home
To put my fears to rout!

The rose may blush and the sun may shine,
The tide ebbs slowly out;
The world is good if you are mine,
Ashes and dust without!

SUNSET SONG

Far off against the solemn sky
Black lie the city's towers;
Before me rustles, dim and dry,
My field of golden flowers.

How thin the wind's cool whisper draws
Through withered leaf and stalk!
Is this the breeze that once would pause
With blossoms bright to talk?

Dark lies the land in twilight sad,
No bird sings in its bowers;
Where is the glory once that clad
My field of golden flowers?

The distant city rings its bells,
Like memory's tender chime;
O sweet, sweet bells, ye speak farewells
To life's enchanted prime!

Dark lies the land in twilight cold,
Gone are the sumptuous hours;
The city sleeps, and shadows fold
My field of golden flowers,

"LOVE SHALL SAVE US ALL"

O Pilgrim, comes the night so fast?
Let not the dark thy heart appall,
Though loom the shadows vague and vast,
For Love shall save us all.

There is no hope hut this to see
Through tears that gather fast and fall;
Too great to perish Love must be,
And Love shall save us all.

Have patience with our loss and pain,
Our troubled space of days so small;
We shall not reach our arms in vain,
For Love shall save us all.

O Pilgrim, but a moment wait,
And we shall hear our darlings call
Beyond death's mute and awful gate,
And Love shall save us all!

THE CRUISE OF THE MYSTERY

The children wandered up and down,
Seeking for driftwood o'er the sand;
The elder tugged at granny's gown,
And pointed with his little hand.

"Look! look!" he cried, "at yonder ship
That sails so fast and looms so tall!"
She turned, and let her basket slip,
And all her gathered treasure fall.

"Nay, granny, why are you so pale?
Where is the ship we saw but now?"
"Oh, child, it was no mortal sail!
It came and went, I know not how.

"But ill winds fill that canvas white
That blow no good to you and me.
Oh, woe for us who saw the sight
That evil bodes to all who see!"

They pressed about her, all afraid:
"Oh, tell us, granny, what was she?"
"A ship's unhappy ghost," she said,
"The awful ship, the Mystery."

"But tell us, tell us!" "Quiet be!"
She said. "Sit close and listen well,
For what befell the Mystery
It is a fearful thing to tell! "

She was a slave-ship long ago.
Year after year across the sea
She made a trade of human woe,
And carried freights of misery.

One voyage, when from the tropic coast
Laden with dusky forms she came, —
A wretched and despairing host, —

Beneath the fierce sun's breathless flame

Sprang, like a wild beast from its lair,
The fury of the hurricane,
And sent the great ship reeling bare
Across the roaring ocean plain.

Then terror seized the piteous crowd:
With many an oath and cruel blow
The captain drove them, shrieking loud,
Into the pitch-black hold below.

Shouting, "Make fast the hatchways tight!"
He cursed them: "Let them live or die,
They 'll trouble us no more to-night! "
The crew obeyed him sullenly.

Has hell such torment as they knew?
Like herded cattle packed they lay,
Till morning showed a streak of blue
Breaking the sky's thick pall of gray.

"Off with the hatchways, men!" No sound!
What sound should rise from out a grave?
The silence shook with dread profound
The heart of every seaman brave.

"Quick! Drag them up," the captain said,
"And pitch the dead into the sea! "
The sea was peopled with the dead,
With wide eyes staring fearfully.

From weltering wave to wave they tossed.
Two hundred corpses, stiff and stark,
At last were in the distance lost,
A banquet for the wandering shark.

Oh, sweetly the relenting day
Changed, till the storm had left no trace,
And the whole awful ocean lay
As tranquil as an infant's face.

Abaft the wind hauled fair and fine,
Lightly the ship sped on her way;
Her sharp bows crushed the yielding brine
Into a diamond dust of spray.

But up and down the decks her crew

Shook their rough heads, and eyed askance,
With doubt and hate that ever grew,
The captain's brutal countenance,

As slow he paced with frown as black
As night. At last, with sudden shout,
He turned. "'Bout ship! We will go back
And fetch another cargo out!"

They put the ship about again;
His will was law, they could not choose.
They strove to change her course in vain:
Down fell the wind, the sails hung loose,

And from the far horizon dim
An oily calm crept silently
Over the sea from rim to rim;
Still as if anchored fast lay she.

The sun set red, the moon shone white,
On idle canvas drooping drear;
Through the vast, solemn hush of night
What is it that the sailors hear?

Now do they sleep — and do they dream?
Was that the wind's foreboding moan?
From stem to stern her every beam
Quivered with one unearthly groan!

Leaped to his feet then every man,
And shuddered, clinging to his mate;
And sunburned cheeks grew pale and wan,
Blanched with that thrill of terror great.

The captain waked, and angrily
Sprang to the deck, and cursing spoke.
"What devil's trick is this? n cried he.
No answer the scared silence broke.

But quietly the moonlight clear
Sent o'er the waves its pallid glow:
What stirred the water far and near,
With stealthy motion swimming slow?

With measured strokes those swimmers dread
From every side came gathering fast;
The sea was peopled with the dead
That to its cruel deeps were cast!

And coiling, curling, crawling on,
The phantom troop pressed nigh and nigher,
And every dusky body shone
Outlined in phosphorescent fire.

They gained the ship, they climbed the shrouds,
They swarmed from keel to topmast high:
Now here, now there, like filmy clouds
Without a sound they flickered by.

And where the captain stood aghast,
With hollow, mocking eyes they came,
And bound him fast unto the mast
With ghostly ropes that bit like flame.

Like maniacs shrieked the startled crew!
They loosed the boats, they leaped within;
Before their oars the water flew;
They pulled as if some race to win.

With spectral light all gleaming bright
The Mystery in the distance lay;
Away from that accursed sight
They fled until the break of day.

And they were rescued, but the ship,
The awful ship, the Mystery,
Her captain in the dead men's grip, —
Never to any port came she;

But up and down the roaring seas
For ever and for aye she sails,
In calm or storm, against the breeze,
Unshaken by the wildest gales.

And wheresoe'er her form appears
Come trouble and disaster sore,
And she has sailed a hundred years,
And she will sail for evermore.

SCHUMANN'S SONATA IN A MINOR

(mit leidenschaftlichem ausdruck)

The quiet room, the flowers, the perfumed calm,

The slender crystal vase, where all aflame
The scarlet poppies stand erect and tall,
Color that burns as if no frost could tame,
The shaded lamplight glowing over all,
The summer night a dream of warmth and balm.

Outbreaks at once the golden melody,
"With passionate expression!" Ah, from whence
Comes the enchantment of this potent spell,
This charm that takes us captive, soul and sense!
The sacred power of music, who shall tell,
Who find the secret of its mastery?

Lo, in the keen vibration of the air
Pierced by the sweetness of the violin,
Shaken by thrilling chords and searching notes
That flood the ivory keys, the flowers begin
To tremble; 'tis as if some spirit floats
And breathes upon their beauty unaware.

The stately poppies, proud in stillness, stand
In silken splendor of superb attire:
Stricken with arrows of melodious sound,
Their loosened petals fall like flakes of fire;
With waves of music overwhelmed and drowned,
Solemnly drop their flames on either hand.

So the rich moment dies, and what is left?
Only a memory sweet, to shut between
Some poem's silent leaves, to find again,
Perhaps, when winter blasts are howling keen,
And summer's loveliness is spoiled and slain,
And all the world of light and bloom bereft.

But winter cannot rob the music so!
Nor time nor fate its subtle power destroy
To bring again the summer's dear caress,
To wake the heart to youth's unreasoning joy, —
Sound, color, perfume, love, to warm and bless,
And airs of balm from Paradise that blow.

BECAUSE OF THEE

My life has grown so dear to me
Because of thee!
My maiden with the eyes demure,

And quiet mouth, and forehead pure,
Joy makes a summer in my heart
Because thou art!

The very winds melodious be
Because of thee!
The rose is sweeter for thy sake,
The waves in softer music break,
On brighter wings the swallows dart,
Because thou art!

My sky is swept of shadows free
Because of thee!
Sorrow and care have lost their sting,
The blossoms glow, the linnets sing,
All things in my delight have part,
Because thou art!

FLOWERS FOR THE BRAVE

(Decoration Day, 1883)

Here bring your purple and gold,
Glory of color and scent;
Scarlet of tulips bold,
Buds blue as the firmament.

Hushed is the sound of the fife
And the bugle piping clear.
The vivid and delicate life
In the soul of the youthful year

We bring to the quiet dead,
With a gentle and tempered grief:
O'er the mounds so mute we shed
The beauty of blossom and leaf.

The flashing swords that were drawn,
No rust shall their fame destroy!
Boughs rosy as rifts of dawn,
Like the blush on the cheek of joy,

Rich fires of the gardens and meads
We kindle, these hearts above!
What splendor can match their deeds?
What sweetness can match our love?

EXPOSTULATION

Tears in those eyes of blue!
Sparks of fiery dew,
Scornful lightnings that flash
'Twixt dusky lash and lash!
Never from sorrow grew
That rain in my heaven of blue.

Full of disdain are you,
Scorn for these fetters new.
Sweet, you were free too long!
Love is a master strong,
Hard are the words but true,
None may his chain undo.

Nay! Let your heart shine through
And soften those eyes of blue!
Glide from your chilly height,
Banish your anger bright;
Fairest, be gentlest, too,
Fate is too mighty for you!

PERSISTENCE

Skeleton schooner, looming strange on the far horizon's rim,
Wasted and blurred by the bitter cold, all ghastly and pallid and dim,
Whither goest thou, stiff and stark? What harbor locked in the frost
Steerest thou for, through the freezing spray by the hissing breakers tossed?

Wherefore strivest thou, fighting still to plough thy perilous way
Against the might of the fierce northwest so woefully, night and day?
Turn thee and spread thy wings so white, and fly to the tropic seas,
Till the clogging ice that loads thee now dissolves in a torrid breeze;

Till the blazing sun shall melt the tar in every rope and seam;
Till thy frozen keel warm tides shall rock in a languid, lovely dream;
Till thou liest lapped in perfumes sweet in some palm-girdled bay,
Anchored in peace, to rest at last, for many a golden day.

What cheer can be in thy dreadful toil, what hope in the raging deep?
What joy from out their troubled voyage can thy worn seamen reap?
Loosen thy close-reefed canvas, then, fling wide thy pinions white,

Leap the long billows, swiftly sail into the south' s delight!

Steadfast she steers to the bitter north along the horizon's rim,
Wasted and blurred by the cruel cold, dull, ghostly, and pallid, and dim;
For grand are the will and courage of man, and still she must keep her course,
And though she perish still must fight against nature's terrible force.

S. E.

She passes up and down life's various ways
With noiseless footfall and with serious air:
Within the circle of her quiet days
She takes of sorrow and of joy her share.
In her bright home, like some rare jewel set,
The lustre of her beauty lives and glows,
With all the fragrance of the violet,
And all the radiant splendor of the rose.
As simple and unconscious as a flower,
And crowned with womanhood's most subtle charm,
She blesses her sweet realm with gentle power,
And keeps her hearth-fires burning clear and warm.
To know her is to love her. Every year
Makes her more precious and more wise and dear.

POOR LISETTE

Sadly the quails in the cornland pipe,
Yellow the harvest is bending ripe,
Gayly the children each other greet,
Wandering down through the village street.

By her garden gate leans poor Lisette.
"Her lover," they whisper, "comes not yet."
She looks afar to the edge of the sky,
Where blue and misty the mountains lie.

What sudden echoes of fife and drum
Down the long, dim, winding valley come!
Oh, bring they news for the poor Lisette,
Rapture at last, or a life's regret?

High ring the bugle notes so sweet,
Nearer the rhythmic tramp of feet, —
What tempest rushes to clasp Lisette,

With lips so warm and with eyes so wet!

She is safe in her lover's arms at last;
A dreary dream is the wretched past;
The music of joy in her glad heart plays,
And morning dawns in her radiant face:

While clearly the quails in the cornland pipe,
And silent the harvest is bending ripe,
And the children shout to the fife and drum
That pain is over and peace is come.

TO J. G. W.

ON HIS SEVENTY-FIFTH BIRTHDAY

What is there left, I wonder,
To give thee on this glad day?
Vainly I muse and ponder;
What is there left to say?

There is winter abroad, and snow,
And winds that are chill and drear
Over the sad earth blow,
Like the sighs of the dying year.

But the land thou lovest is warm
At heart with the love of thee,
And breaks into bloom and charm
And fragrance, that thou mayest see.

Violet, laurel, and rose,
They are laid before thy feet,
And the red rose deeper glows
At a fate so proud and sweet.

Gifts and greeting and blessing,
Honor and praise, are thine;
There 's naught left worth expressing
By any word or sign!

So, like the rest, I offer
The gift all gifts above
That heaven or earth can proffer, —
Deep, gentle, grateful, love.

IN TUSCANY

Down San Miniato in the afternoon
Slowly we drove through still and golden air.
'T was winter, but the day was soft as June;
Florence was spread beneath us, passing fair.

The matchless city! Set about with flowers,
Peaceful along her Arno's banks she lay;
Her treasured splendors, roofs and domes and towers,
In tender light of the Italian day.

Sweet breathed the roses, glowing far and wide,
Pink, gold, ''and crimson; dark in stately gloom
Stood the thick cypresses; on every side
The laurestinus, rich with creamy bloom.

And exquisite, pale, sharp-leaved olives grew
In moonlight colors, silver-green and gray,
While, lifting their proud heads high in the blue,
Sprang the superb stone-pines beside the way.

Oh, wonderful, I thought, beyond compare!
And hushed with pleasure silent sat and gazed,
When lo! a child's voice, and I grew aware
Of loveliness that left me all amazed.

A little beggar girl, that leaping came
Forth from the roadside, reaching out her hand,
And dancing like a bright and buoyant flame,
Besought us in the music of her land.

Her eyes were like a midnight full of stars
Below the dazzling beauty of her brows,
Her dusky hair dark as the cloud that bars
The moon in troubled skies when tempests rouse;

A mouth where lightning- sweet the sudden smile
Came, went and came, and flashed into my face,
And caught my heart, as, holding fast the while
The carriage edge, she ran with rapid grace.

Who could withstand her pleading, who resist
The magic of those love-compelling eyes,
Those lips the red pomegranate flowers had kissed,
The voice that charmed like woven melodies!

Not we! Surely, I thought, imperial blood,
Some priceless current from a kingly line,
Ran royal in her veins, — a sunny flood
That marked her with its fine, mysterious sign.

She was not born to ask, but to command;
She seemed to crown the wonder of the day,
The perfect blossom of that glorious land,
While her sweet "Grazie!" followed on our way,

As down 'mid olive, cypress, stately pine,
Among the roses in a dream we passed,
Through glamour of the time and place divine,
Till Arno's quiet banks were reached at last,

And pleasant rest. 'T is years since those fair hours,
But their rich memories live, their sun and shade,
Beautiful Florence set about with flowers,
And San Miniato's peerless beggar maid.

GOOD-BY, SWEET DAY

FOR MUSIC

Good-by, sweet day, good-by!
I have so loved thee, but I cannot hold thee.
Departing like a dream, the shadows fold thee;
Slowly thy perfect beauty fades away:
Good-by, sweet day!

Good-by, sweet day, good-by!
Dear were thy golden hours of tranquil splendor,
Sadly thou yieldest to the evening tender
Who wert so fair from thy first morning ray;
Good-by, sweet day!

Good-by, sweet day, good-by!
Thy glow and charm, thy smiles and tones and glances,
Vanish at last, and solemn night advances;
Ah, couldst thou yet a little longer stay!
Good-by, sweet day!

Good-by, sweet day, good-by!
All thy rich gifts my grateful heart remembers,
The while I watch thy sunset's smouldering embers

Die in the west beneath the twilight gray.
Good-by, sweet day!

IN AUTUMN

The aster by the brook is dead,
And quenched the goldenrod's brief fire;
The maple's last red leaf is shed,
And dumb the birds' sweet choir.

'T is life's November, too. How swift
The narrowing days speed, one by one!
How pale the waning sunbeams sift
Through clouds of gray and dun!

And as we lose our wistful hold
On warmth and loveliness and youth,
And shudder at the dark and cold,
Our souls cry out for Truth.

No more mirage, O Heavenly Powers,
To mock our sight with shows so fair!
We question of the solemn hours
That lead us swiftly — "Where ?"

We hunger for our lost — in vain!
We lift our close-clasped hands above,
And pray God's pity on our pain,
And trust the Eternal Love.

WEST-WIND

The barley bows from the west
Before the delicate breeze
That many a sail caressed
As it swept the sapphire seas.

It has found the garden sweet,
And the poppy's cup it sways',
Bends the golden ears of wheat;
And its dreamy touch it lays

On the heavy mignonette,
Stealing soft its odors fine,

On the pansies dewy yet,
On the phloxes red as wine.

Where the honeysuckle sweet
Storms the sunny porch with flowers,
Like a tempest of delight
Shaking fragrance down in showers,

It touches with airy grace
Each clustering, perfumed spray,
Clasps all in a light embrace,
And silently wanders away.

Come forth in the air divine,
Thou dearest, my crown of bliss!
Give that flower-sweet cheek of thine
To the morning breeze to kiss.

Add but thy perfect presence
To gladden my happy eyes,
And I would not change earth's morning
For the dawns of Paradise!

IMPATIENCE

E. L.

Only to follow you, dearest, only to find you!
Only to feel for one instant the touch of your hand;
Only to tell you once of the love you left behind you, —
To say the world without you is like a desert of sand;

That the flowers have lost their perfume, the rose its splendor,
And the charm of nature is lost in a dull eclipse;
That joy went out with the glance of your eyes so tender,
And beauty passed with the lovely smile on your lips.

I did not dream it was you who kindled the morning
And folded the evening purple in peace so sweet;
But you took the whole world's rapture without a warning,
And left me naught save the print of your patient feet.

I count the days and the hours that hold us asunder:
I long for Death's friendly hand which shall rend in twain,
With the glorious lightning flash and the golden thunder,
These clouds of the earth, and give me my own again!

By cottage walls the lilacs blow;
Rich spikes of perfume stand and sway
At open casements, where all day
The warm wind waves them to and fro.

Out of the shadow of the door,
Into the golden morning air,
Comes one who makes the day more fair
And summer sweeter than before.

The apple blossoms might have shed
Upon her cheek the bloom so rare;
The sun has kissed her bright brown hair
Braided about her graceful head.

Lightly betwixt the lilacs tall
She passes, through the garden gate,
Across the road, and stays to wait
A moment by the orchard wall;

And then in gracious light and shade,
Beneath the blossom-laden trees,
'Mid song of birds and hum of bees,
She strays, unconscious, unafraid,

Till swiftly o'er the grassy space
Comes one whose step she fain would stay.
Glad as the newly risen day
He stoops to read her drooping face.

Her face is like the morning skies,
Bright, timid, tender, blushing sweet;
She dares not trust her own to meet
The steady splendor of his eyes.

He holds her with resistless charm,
With truth, with power, with beauty crowned;
About her lovely shape is wound
The strong, safe girdle of his arm.

And up and down through shade and light
They wander through the flying hours,
And all the way is strewn with flowers,

And life looks like one long delight.

Ah, happy twain! No frost shall harm,
No change shall reach your bliss, so long
As keeps its place the faithful, strong,
Safe girdle of that folding arm.

Could you this simple secret know
No death in life would be to fear,
When you may watch, in some sad year,
By cottage walls the lilacs blow!

HER MIRROR

O mirror, whence her lovely face
Was wont to look with radiance sweet,
Hast thou not kept of her some trace,
Some memory that thou mayest repeat?

Could I but find in thee once more
Some token of her presence dear!
O mirror, wilt thou not restore
Her shadow for an instant here?

Thou couldst not yield a boon so great.
I see my own dim face and eyes
With love and longing desolate,
All drowned in wistful memories.

Blindly for her dear hand I grope;
There's nothing life can have in store
So sweet to me as this sweet hope,
To feel her smile on me once more!

FOR CHRISTMAS

"Thy own wish wish I thee in every place."
The Christmas joy, the song, the feast, the cheer,
Thine be the light of love in every face
That looks on thee, to bless thy coming year.

Thy own wish wish I thee. What dost thou crave?
All thy dear hopes be thine, whate'er they be.
A wish fulfilled may make thee king or slave;

I wish thee Wisdom's eyes wherewith to see.

Behold, she stands and waits, the youthful year!
A breeze of morning breathes about her brows;
She holds thy storm and sunshine, bliss and fear,
Blossom and fruit upon the bending boughs.

She brings thee gifts. What blessing wilt thou choose?
Life's crown of good in earth or heaven above,
The one immortal joy thou canst not lose,
Is Love! Leave all the rest, and choose thou Love!

AT SET OF MOON

The wind blows from the stormy quarter and the moon is old.
Trouble has gathered in the sky so pallid, dim, and cold.
Can this be morning? Is the world so blank and out of tune?
Down yonder dim horizon something fades beside the moon.

What is it? 'Tis the ghost of joy that made the earth so sweet;
Life's one supreme, bright happiness, that hastes with flying feet.
The fading moon will brighten soon, in splendor shine again,
But joy that was the life of life is merged in bitter pain.

Last night I passed her window: she dreamed not I was near.
One ray slipped through the jealous curtain, rosy-warm and clear;
I kissed the flowers on which it fell, all dewy cold were they.
With patient anguish in my heart I turned and stole away.

She will not miss me, will not know if I am here or there;
If I am dead, or if I live, will neither know nor care.
Death is not bitter as my grief, which craves one single boon, —
Release me, God! let my life fade like yonder waning moon.

MY GARDEN

It blossomed by the summer sea,
A tiny space of tangled bloom
Wherein so many flowers found room,
A miracle it seemed to be!

Up from the ground, alert and bright,
The pansies laughed in gold and jet,
Purple and pied, and mignonette

Breathed like a spirit of delight.

Flaming the rich nasturtiums ran
Along the fence, and marigolds
"Opened afresh their starry folds"
In beauty as the day began;

While ranks of scarlet poppies gay
Waved when the soft south-wind did blow,
Superb in sunshine, to and fro,
Like soldiers proud in brave array.

And tall blue larkspur waved its spikes
Against the sea's deep violet,
That every breeze makes deeper yet
With splendid azure where it strikes;

And rosy-pale sweet-peas climbed up,
And phloxes spread their colors fine,
Pink, white, and purple, red as wine,
And fire burned in the eschscholtzia's cup.

More dear to me than words can tell
Was every cup and spray and leaf;
Too perfect for a life so brief
Seemed every star and bud and bell.

And many a maiden, fairer yet,
Came smiling to my garden gay,
Whose graceful head I decked alway
With pansy and with mignonette.

Such slender shapes of girlhood young
Haunted that little blooming space,
Each with a more delightful face
Than any flower that ever sprung!

O shadowy shapes of youthful bloom!
How fair the sweet procession glides
Down memory's swift and silent tides,
Till lost in doubtful mists of gloom!

Year after year new flowers unfold,
Year after year fresh maidens fair,
Scenting their perfume on the air,
Follow and find their red and gold.

And while for them the poppies' blaze

I gather, brightening into mine
The eyes of vanished beauty shine,
That gladdened long-lost summer days.

Where are they all who wide have ranged?
Where are the flowers of other years?
What ear the wistful question hears?
Ah, some are dead and all are changed.

And still the constant earth renews
Her treasured splendor; still unfold
Petals of purple and of gold
Beneath the sunshine and the dews.

But for her human children dear
Whom she has folded to her breast,
No beauty wakes them from their rest,
Nor change they with the changing year.

LOST AND SAVED

"O Love," he whispered low, "Eternal Love!"
And softly twilight's shadows round them drew,
And one by one the stars grew bright above,
And warm airs from the gates of sunset blew.

Swift o'er the summer sea they lightly sailed;
The rushing winds, the rushing waves, sang sweet;
But sweeter than all sounds the voice that failed,
Shaken by the full heart that strongly beat.

Fast piled the clouds in darkness south and east,
Each other's starry eyes they only saw.
What was the world to them? The breeze increased,
And caught the glimmering sail with gusty flaw.

Low stooped the mast; the firm hand at the helm
Held bravely yet the light craft to its course,
Though hurrying breakers fain would overwhelm,
And the gale gathered with resistless force.

Black night, black storm, that rose in sudden wrath!
All lost the cheerful stars forgot to burn,
And death was waiting silent in the path,
Along whose wavering way was no return.

Or life or death — what mattered it to them?
Locked mute and still within each other's arms,
They sought no more the tempest's rage to stem,
Deaf to the tumult of the night's alarms.

Beyond their fate uplifted, death was naught,
Nor could they know, borne safe all pain above,
Into immortal life together caught,
That only thus should live Eternal Love!

A ROSE OF JOY

FOR A BETROTHAL

As when one wears a fragrant rose
Close to the heart, a rose most fair,
And while the day's life onward flows
Forgets that it is fastened there,

And wonders what delicious charm
Dwells in the air about, and whence
Come the rich wafts of perfume warm
Subtly saluting soul and sense;

And then, remembering what it is,
Bends smiling eyes the flower above,
Adores its beauty and its bliss
And looks on it with grateful love —

Even so I wear, friend of mine,
The sweet thought of your happiness;
The knowledge of your joy divine
Is fragrant with a power to bless.

With the day's work preoccupied
Vaguely, half conscious of delight,
Upborne as on a buoyant tide,
I wonder why life seems so bright.

Then memory speaks; then winter gray
And age and cares that have no end
Touch me no more. I am to-day
Rich in the wealth that cheers my friend.

IN SEPTEMBER

Leaping from the boat, through the lazy, sparkling surf,
Up the slope we press, o'er the rich, elastic turf.
Heavy waves the goldenrod in the morning breeze,
Swift spring the startled grasshoppers, thick about our knees.

Look, how shines the distance! Leagues of water blue,
Wind-swept, sunshine-flooded, with a flying sail or two,
Gleaming white as silver, and dreaming, here and there
A snowy-breasted gull floats in the golden air.

How sweet to climb together the scented, flowery slope,
O dearest, hand in hand, like children following hope;
Laughing at the grasshoppers, singing with delight,
Only to be alive this September morning bright!

But where would be the beauty of this brilliant atmosphere
Wert thou away, my darling? Would not the sky be drear,
And gray the living azure of the changing, sparkling sea?
And blossoms, birds, and sails, and clouds — what would they be to me?

Rest we here a little upon the breezy height,
And watch the play of color, the shadow, and the light,
And let the lovely moment overflow us with its bliss.
When shall we find another so beautiful as this?

I turn from all the splendor to those clear eyes of thine,
That watch the shimmering sails on the far horizon line;
While sun and wind salute thy cheek till roses blossom there,
Thou golden creature, than the morn a thousand times more fair!

Ah! must it end? Must winter hurl its snow across the sea,
And roar with leagues of bitterness between thy face and me?
Must chill December fill with murk and storm this wooing air,
And the west-wind wail like the voice of some supreme despair?

Too surely! But, friendly eyes, hold summer safe for me;
Only, O gentle heart, keep warm and sweet my memory;
And no fury of the tempest my world can desolate —
This winged joy will lift my soul above the storms of fate.

UNDER THE EAVES

Pleasant above the city's din
My quiet room beneath the eaves;

The first to see the day begin,
The last the sunshine lingering leaves.

Pleasant upon the window pane
Uplifted high, so near the sky,
To hear the patter of the rain,
Or see the snow go swirling by;

To watch the gilded weathercocks
In every eddy turn and wheel;
To hear the clear, melodious shocks
Of chiming bells that clang and peal.

Dove-haunted roofs and towers and spires,
The friendly faces of the clocks,
The network of electric wires,
The sparrows gossiping in flocks,

The smoke's dim, ragged phantoms soft
Prom myriad chimneys lightly curled,
That mingle with the clouds aloft
Slow sailing with the sailing world —

Pleasant and peaceful all. Most sweet
When morning and when evening fires,
Silent above the busy street,
Touch the dove-haunted roofs and spires.

Neighbored by sparrow and by dove,
A comrade of the weathercocks,
My quiet, airy perch I love,
The chimney-stacks, the city clocks;

And thank the heavens that bend above
For leave to find such deep delight
In tower and spire and fluttering dove,
Color and cloud and sparrow's flight.

NOVEMBER MORNING

With clamor the wild southwester
Through the wide heaven is roaring,
Ploughing the ocean, and over
The earth its fury outpouring.

Lo, how the vast gray spaces

Wrestle and roll and thunder,
Billow piled upon billow,
Closing and tearing asunder,

As if the deep raged with the anger
Of hosts of the fabulous kraken!
And the firm house shudders and trembles,
Beaten, buffeted, shaken

Battles the gull with the tempest,
Struggling and wavering and faltering,
Soaring and striving and sinking,
Turning, its high course altering.

Down through the cloudy heaven
Notes from the wild geese are falling;
Cries like harsh hell-tones are ringing,
Echoing, clanging, and calling.

Plunges the schooner landward,
Swiftly the long seas crossing,
Close-reefed, seeking the harbor,
Half lost in the spray she is tossing.

A rift in the roof of vapor!
And stormy sunshine is streaming
To color the gray, wild water
Like chrysoprase, green and gleaming.

Cold and tempestuous ocean,
Ragged rock, brine-swept and lonely,
Grasp of the long, hitter winter —
These things to gladden me only!

Love, dost thou wait for me in some rich land
Where the gold orange hangs in odorous calm?
Where the clear waters kiss the flowery strand,
Bordered with shining sand and groves of palm?

And while this hitter morning creaks for me,
Draws to its close thy warm, delicious day;
Lights, colors, perfumes, music, joy, for thee,
For me the cold, wild sea, the cloudy gray!

Rises the red moon in thy tranquil sky,
Plashes the fountain with its silver talk,
And as the evening wind begins to sigh,
Thy sweet girl's shape steals down the garden walk

And through, the scented dusk a white robe gleams,
Lingering beneath the starry jasmine sprays,
Till where thy clustered roses breathe in dreams,
A sudden gush of song thy light step stays.

That was the nightingale! Love of mine,
Hear'st thou my voice in that pathetic song,
Throbbing in passionate cadences divine,
Sinking to silence with its rapture strong?

I stretch my arms to thee through all the cold,
Through all the dark, across the weary space
Between us, and thy slender form I fold,
And gaze into the wonder of thy face.

Pure brow the moonbeam touches, tender eyes
Splendid with feeling, delicate smiling mouth,
And heavy silken hair that darkly lies
Soft as the twilight clouds in thy sweet South, —

O beautiful my Love! In vain I seek
To hold the heavenly dream that fades from me.
I needs must wake with salt spray on my cheek,
Flung from the fury of this northern sea.

IN DEATH'S DESPITE

Whither departs the perfume of the rose?
Into what life dies music's golden sound?
Year after year life's long procession goes
To hide itself beneath the senseless ground.
Upon the grave's inexorable brink
Amazed with loss the human creature stands;
Vainly he strives to reason or to think,
Left with his aching heart and empty hands;
He calls his lost in vain. In sorrow drowned,
Darkness and silence all his sense confound.

Till in Death's roll-call stern he hears his name,
In turn he follows and is lost to sight;
Though comforted by love and crowned by fame,
He hears the summons dread no man may slight.
Sweetly and clear upon his quiet grave
The birds shall sing, unmindful of his dust;
Softly in turn the long green grass shall wave

Over his fallen head. In turn he must
Submit to be forgotten, like the rest,
Though high the heart that beat within his breast.

The rose falls and the music's sound is gone;
Dear voices cease, and clasp of loving hands;
Alone we stand when the brief day is done,
Searching with saddened eyes earth's darkening lands.
Worthless as is the lightest fallen leaf
We seem, yet constant as the night's first star
Kindles our deathless hope, and from our grief
Is born the trust no misery can mar,
That Love shall lift us all despair above,
Shall conquer death, — yea, Love, and only Love!

A SONG OF HOPE

The morning breaks, the storm is past. Behold!
Along the west the lift grows bright, — the sea
Leaps sparkling blue to catch the sunshine's gold,
And swift before the breeze the vapors flee.

Light cloud-flocks white that troop in joyful haste
Up and across the pure and tender sky;
Light laughing waves that dimple all the waste
And break upon the rocks and hurry by!

Flying of sails, of clouds, a tumult sweet,
Wet, tossing buoys, a warm wild wind that blows
The pennon out and rushes on to greet
Thy lovely cheek and heighten its soft rose!

Beloved, beloved! Is there no morning breeze
To clear our sky and chase our mists away,
Like this great air that sweeps the freshening seas,
And wakes the old sad world to glad new day.

Sweeter than morning, stronger than the gale,
Deeper than ocean, warmer than the sun,
My love shall climb, shall claim thee, shall prevail
Against eternal darkness, dearest one!

OUR SOLDIERS

Peace smiles over hamlet and city,

Peace broods over mountain and stream,
Our tears of anguish and pity
Are a half-forgotten dream.
The tempest of battle is ended,
And our dear, delivered land
Stands free in the sunshine splendid,
No stain upon her hand.

What shall we do to honor
Her dauntless sons to-day,
Who shed such glory upon her,
Striking her chains away?
Fair floats the banner o'er her, —
What did not her children give?
They cast their lives before her,
Dying that she might live.

Remember them, praise them, love them,
The noble hearts and brave!
May earth lie lightly above them
In many a nameless grave.
Great was their high endeavor,
Great is their glorious meed;
Honor our heroes forever,
Praise them with word and deed!

TWO

She turned the letter's rustling page; her smile
Made bright the air about her while she read:
"I come to you to-morrow, love; meanwhile
Love me, my sweet," he said.

"What other business has my life?" she thought,
And musing passed, as in some happy dream,
To the day's care and toils, and while she wrought
Time winged with light did seem.

To-morrow! When the summer morning broke
In rose and gold, and touched her slumbering eyes
Softly, with tempered splendor, and she woke
To the rich dawn's surprise,

Birds sang aloft and roses bloomed below;
Flushed wide the tender fleecy mists above;
Came Memory, leading Hope, and whispered low,

"Love me! I come, my love."

"So that thou comest," she thought, "skies may grow gray,
The sun may fade, the sea with foam blanch white,
Tempest and thunder dread may spoil the day,
But not my deep delight."

O sweet and awful Love! power supreme,
Mighty and sacred, terrible art thou!
Beside thee Life and Death are but a dream;
Before thee all must bow.

When in the west the sunset's crimson flame
Burned low and wasted, and the cool winds blew,
Watching the steadfast sky she heard her name
Breathed in the voice she knew.

Joy shook her heart, nor would its pulse be stilled;
Her fair cheek borrowed swift the sunset's bloom.
A presence beautiful and stately filled
The silence of the room.

"Hast thou no word of welcome?" for indeed
Like some mute marble goddess proud stood she;
She turned. "O king of men!" she cried, "what need
That I should welcome thee?"

Her eyes divine beneath her solemn brows
Met his clear gaze and measured strength for strength.
She drooped, as to the sun the lily bows,
Into his arms at length.

Wide swung heaven's gates for them; no more they knew.
The silent stars looked in, they saw them not.
The slow winds wandered soft through dusk and dew,
But earth was all forgot.

COMPENSATION

In that new world toward which our feet are set,
Shall we find aught to make our hearts forget
Earth's homely joys and her bright hours of bliss?
Has heaven a spell divine enough for this?
Eor who the pleasure of the spring shall tell,
When on the leafless stalk the brown buds swell,
When the grass brightens and the days grow long,

And little birds break out in rippling song?

Oh sweet the dropping eve, the blush of morn,
The starlit sky, the rustling fields of corn,
The soft airs blowing from the freshening seas,
The sun-flecked shadow of the stately trees,
The mellow thunder and the lulling rain,
The warm, delicious, happy summer rain,
When the grass brightens and the days grow long,
And little birds break out in rippling song!

O beauty manifold, from morn till night,
Dawn's flush, noon's blaze, and sunset's tender light!
fair, familiar features, changes sweet
Of her revolving seasons, storm and sleet
And golden calm, as slow she wheels through space
Erom snow to roses, — and how dear her face
When the grass brightens and the days grow long,
And little birds break out in rippling song!

O happy Earth! home so well beloved!
What recompense have we, from thee removed?
One hope we have that overtops the whole, —
The hope of finding every vanished soul
We love and long for daily, and for this
Gladly we turn from thee and all thy bliss,
Even at thy loveliest, when the days are long,
And little birds break out in rippling song.

SONNET

Back from life's coasts the ebbing tide had drawn,
The singing tide that brimmed with joy the shore:
The torch of sunset and the blush of dawn
Seemed to have lost their glow forevermore,
There was such silence in the empty sky!
And Nature mocked me, grown so cold and dumb,
And Faith, I thought, had perished utterly,
Nor knew I whence a ray of hope should come;
When, like a royal messenger of good
Sent to some sad and famine-stricken land,
Across my threshold dark you passed, and stood,
Bearing the keys of heaven in your hand;
And wide the bright, resounding gates you threw!
Tell me, friend, what I shall do for you!

JOY

Joy breathes in the sweet airs of spring,
And in the shy wild blossom hides,
And soars upon the swallow's wing,
And with the singing water glides.

Where lilies stand, a fragrant crowd,
Rocked by the warm south wind he lies;
And dreams upon the balmy cloud
Soft floating in the tender skies;

Shines clear from out the crescent sharp,
Glittering above the sunset's red,
And of the west wind makes a harp,
And gleams in starlight overhead.

Joy mantles in the golden wine,
Joy to earth's humblest doth descend,
And looks at me with cheer divine
From out the dear eyes of my friend.

BELOVED

A strong sweet tide toward the lonely shore
Sets steadfastly, till every inlet sings,
And to the waiting silence, blank before,
Its full refreshment brings.

Through the day's business passing to and fro,
Ever she grows more conscious of the charm
Upholding her wherever she may go,
Like some enfolding arm.

For this dear joy all days more fair do seem,
The night's repose more blissful and more deep,
As pillowed on the breast of this sweet dream
Softly she falls asleep.

Safe is she, lifted all earth's ills above;
No storm can break her calm, no evil reach
Within the charmed circle drawn by Love,
Blest beyond thought or speech.

O maiden, dream thy dream! Life's crown of thorns,
Draws it not down, unseen, about thy brows?
The glory of thy summer eves and morns
Stern winter shall espouse.

Within this Eden of thy sweet content
No mortal stays, — that, the great gods forbid;
But canst thou learn that in thy banishment
A higher good lies hid?

THE ANSWER

The blossoms blush on the bough,
And the air is full of song,
Oh give me my answer now,
Dear Love, I have waited long!

The blossoms mantle and flush, —
I see but the rose in your cheek, —
And the birds their music hush,
For the fate your lips may speak.

I listen for life or death,
With hope's deep rapture stirred,
And faint as the blossoms' breath
Comes your low, delicious word.

And the earth reels under my feet, —
blossoms that burn on the bough! —
With the strength of a joy so sweet,
For I have my answer now!

SONG

Past the point and by the beach,
Oh but the waves ran merrily,
With laughter light and silver speech,
And red the sunset flushed the sea.

Two lovers wandered side by side, —
Oh but the waves ran merrily;
They watched the rushing of the tide,
And fairer than a dream was she.

About her slender waist was cast —
Oh but the waves ran merrily —
His strong right arm that held her fast,
A zone that clasped her royally.

He gazed in her bewildering face, —
Oh but the waves ran merrily:
"See how the waves each other chase!
So follow all my thoughts to thee."

"And seest thou yonder star?" she said, —
Oh but the waves ran merrily, —
"Superb in yonder evening-red?
So dost thou light my life for me! "

'Twas long ago that star did shine, —
Oh but the waves ran merrily;
Love made for them the world divine
In that old time beside the sea.

The soft wind sighs, the great sea rolls, —
Oh but the waves run merrily;
What has Time done with those two souls?
And Love, who charmed them, where is he?

AUGUST

Buttercup nodded and said good-by,
Clover and daisy went off together,
But the fragrant water-lilies lie
Yet moored in the golden August weather.

The swallows chatter about their flight,
The cricket chirps like a rare good fellow,
The asters twinkle in clusters bright,
While the corn grows ripe and the apples mellow.

SONG

A bird upon, a rosy bough
Sang low and long, sang late and loud,
Until the young moon's silver prow
Was lost behind a bar of cloud.

The south wind paused and held its breath -
Sing loud and late, sing low and long —
While sweet as Love and sad as Death
The matchless notes rose wild and strong.

They rang with rapture, loss and change, —
Sing low and late, sing long and loud —
A tumult passionate and strange,
A speechless grief, a patience proud;

Till with "farewell for evermore," —
Sing late and loud, sing low and long, —
Like waves that kiss a barren shore
In sobbing cadence died the song.

"OH TELL ME NOT OF HEAVENLY HALLS'

Oh tell me not of heavenly halls,
Of streets of pearl and gates of gold,
Where angel unto angel calls
'Mid splendors of the sky untold;

My homesick heart would backward turn
To find this dear, familiar earth,
To watch its sacred hearth-fires burn,
To catch its songs of joy or mirth.

I 'd lean from out the heavenly choir
To hear once more the red cock crow,
What time the morning's rosy fire
O'er hill and field began to glow.

To hear the ripple of the rain,
The summer waves at ocean's brim,
To hear the sparrow sing again
I 'd quit the wide-eyed cherubim!

I care not what heaven's glories are;
Content am I. More joy it brings
To watch the dandelion's star
Than mystic Saturn's golden rings.

And yet — and yet, dearest one!
My comfort from life's earliest breath —
To follow thee where thou art gone
Through those dim, awful gates of Death,

To find thee, feel thy smile again,
To have eternity's long day
To tell my grateful love, — why, then,
Both heaven and earth might pass away!

MIDSUMMER

White as a blossom is the kerchief quaint
Over her sumptuous shoulders lightly laid;
Fairer than any picture men could paint,
In the cool orchard's fragrant light and shade

She stands and waits: some pensive dream enfolds
Her beauty sweet, and bows her radiant head;
The delicate pale roses that she holds
Seem to have borrowed of her cheek their red.

She waits like some superb but drooping flower
To feel the touch of morning and the sun,
And o'er her head the glowing petals shower,
And to her feet the shifting sunbeams run.

I follow to her feet their pathway fine,
And while my voice the charmed silence breaks,
What startled splendors from her deep eyes shine!
Into what glory my rich flower awakes!

NEW YEAR SONG

O Sorrow, go thy way and leave me!
Weary am I of thee, thou Sorrow old.
Unclasp thy hand from mine and cease to grieve me,
Fade like the winter sunset dim and cold.

Depart, and trouble me no longer!
Die! Vanish with forgotten yesterdays.
Eastward the darkness melts, the light grows stronger,
And dawn breaks sweet across the shrouding haze.

Die and depart, Old Year, old Sorrow!
Welcome, O morning air of health and strength!
glad New Year, bring us new hope to-morrow,
With blossom, leaf, and fruitage bright at length.

CAPTURED

Nanette!
Can you not teach me to forget?
It is so hard to understand!
You would not lift your slender hand
To keep me yours, yet must I be
Yours only, yours eternally,
Though 'neath the chain I strive and fret s
Nanette!

That golden hour when first we met,
Like the swift inundating sea
Love's tide swept in and conquered me.
Love uttered Love's supremest word,
A moment you were touched and stirred;
Ah, that's the anguish of regret,
Nanette!

My every thought on you was set;
I poured for you Love's priceless wine,
You could no more its power divine
Than one small blossom's cup of gold
The boundless firmament could hold:
My eyes with scornful tears are wet,
Nanette!

This withered spray of mignonette
You gave me, from my heart I take,
This sick, sad heart you taught to ache,
And fling it in the restless sea —
I would my thought of you could be
So flung away from me; and yet,
Nanette!

I cannot break the cruel net,
Though I may curse my fate and swear
You are not kind, nor good, nor fair,
You 'll hold me by one silken tress,
Or eyelid's down-dropped loveliness,
A touch of hand, or tone of voice,
Or smile that all my will destroys:
Ah Heaven! the only boon I crave
Is rest, the silence of the grave.
Release me! Teach me to forget,

Nanette!

FAITH

Fain would I hold my lamp of life aloft
Like yonder tower built high above the roof;
Steadfast, though tempests rave or winds blow soft,
Clear, though the sky dissolve in tears of grief.

For darkness passes, storms shall not abide.
A little patience and the fog is past.
After the sorrow of the ebbing tide
The singing flood returns in joy at last.

The night is long and pain weighs heavily,
But God will hold his world above despair.
Look to the East, where up the lucid sky
The morning climbs! The day shall yet be fair 1

AT DAWN

Early this morning waking,
I heard the sandpipers call,
And the sea on the shore was breaking
With a dreamy rise and fall.

The dawn that was softly blushing
Touched cloud and wave with rose,
And the sails in the west were flushing,
No breeze stirred their repose.

What tone in the water's falling
Had reached me while I dreamed?
What sound in the wild birds' calling
Like a heavenly greeting seemed?

What meant the delicate splendor
That brightened the conscious morn
With a radiance fresh and tender
Crowning the day newborn?

All nature's musical voices
Whispered, "Awake and see!
Awake, for the day rejoices!"

What news had the morn for me?

Then I remembered the blessing
So sweet, friend, so near!
The joy beyond all expressing, —
To-day you would be here.

IN A HORSE-CAR

I wondered what power possessed the place
As I took my seat in the motley crowd,
And glancing swiftly from face to face
Of the poor and mean, and the rich and proud,

And all the stages betwixt the two
That daily travel the iron track,
I stopped at a young face fresh as dew,
Framed in white with a hood of black.

'T was a little Sister of Charity;
Oh young and slender, oh sweet and calm!
Like a pensive moonbeam pale was she,
With her fair hands folded palm to palm.

And a delicate beauty of high repose,
A sacred peace, as if far withdrawn
From the hard world's din, like a cloistered rose,
She blossomed pure as the breath of dawn.

I marveled much how a girl like this
In her May time splendor could turn away
From the brimming cup of her youth's bright bliss,
To succor the sorrowful day by day.

And yet when I looked at her once more,
With her lofty aspect of tempered cheer,
All the joys of the earth seemed vain and poor
To the lovely record written here.

And I felt how true it is, how sure
That every good deed adds a light
To the human face, not there before,
While every ill thing leaves its blight.

It does not follow that women and men
Must live in a cloister to work for God;

There's enough to do, to the dullest ken,
In the great world's paths spread wide abroad.

And the good or ill of the life we lead
Is sculptured clear on the countenance;
Be it love and goodness, or sin and greed,
Who runs may read at a single glance.

A VALENTINE

What is the whole world worth, Dear,
Weighed against love and truth?
Sweet is the spring to the earth, Dear,
Bright is the blossom of youth:

And the skies of summer are tender
In fullness of life and strength,
And rich is the autumn splendor,
But winter comes at length.

Tell me, what spell shall charm us
When the golden days expire?
What is there left to warm us
Save Love's most sacred fire?

While on the soul's high altar
Its clear light burns secure,
Though the step of joy may falter,
And the glad years are no more,

The frosts of age are naught, Dear!
I clasp thy hand in mine
Fondly as when youth sought, Dear,
To be thy Valentine,

WITHIN AND WITHOUT

The tide flows up, the tide flows down:
The water brims the creek and falls;
A cottage weather-stained and brown
Lifts at the brink its time-worn walls.

Beneath the lowly window sill
Two little beds of blossoms gay

The wandering airs with fragrance fill,
Sweeten the night and charm the day.

The tide flows up, the tide flows down:
From the low window's humble square
A woman in a faded gown,
With care-dimmed eyes and tangled hair,

Looks out across the smiling space
Where golden suns and stars unfold:
Blue larkspur, the pied pansy's face,
Nasturtium bells of scarlet bold, —

She sees them not. nor cares, nor knows.
A man's rough figure noon and night
And morning o'er the threshold goes, —
No sense has he for their delight.

The tide flows up, the tide flows down:
In that dull house a little maid
Lives lonely, under Fortune's frown,
A life unchildlike and afraid.

To her that tiny garden-plot
Means heaven. She conies at eve to stand
'Mid mallow and forget-me-not
And marigolds on either hand.

They look at her with brilliant eyes,
Their scent is greeting and caress;
They spread their rich and glowing dyes
Her saddened soul to cheer and bless.

The tide flows up, the tide flows down:
Within, how base the life and poor!
Without, what wealth and beauty crown
The humble flowers beside the door!

BETROTHED

Softly the flickering firelight comes and goes;
The warm glow flashes, sinks, departs, returns,
And shows me where the delicate red rose
In the tall, slender vase of crystal burns.

The tempest beats without. The hush within

Is sweeter for the turmoil of the night;
Ice clatters at the pane and snowflakes spin
A web of woven storm, a shroud of white.

Its secret the wild winter weather keeps,
No sound transpires except the tempest's breath;
I orked in the frost the muffled pathway sleeps,
For any human token still as death

My eyes the room's familiar aspect hold,
Its quiet beauty and its sumptuous gloom,
Its glimmering draperies of dull rich gold,
The gleam upon the burnished peacock's plume.

My rose, my book, my work, I see them all,
With my whole soul surrendered to one sense,
My life within my ears, for one footfall
Listening with patience breathless and intense.

'T is my heart hears, at last, the silent door
Swing on its hinges, there's no need the fire
Should show me whose step thrills the conscious floor,
As suddenly the wayward flame leaps higher.

Thou comest, bringing all good things that are!
Infinite joy, and peace with white wings furled,
All heaven is here and thou the morning- star,
Thou splendor of my life! " Thou Day o' the world! n

QUESTIONS

The steadfast planet spins through space,
And into darkness, into light
Swiftly it wheels its living face:
"'T is day," we say, or "It is night."

And we who cling and with it turn,
Till spent is our brief span of years,
Watching our sister stars that burn
Through the dim trouble of our tears,

We question of the silence vast,
Of souls that people distant spheres;
What of their future and their past?
Have they our sorrows, joys, and fears?

Do the same flowers make glad their sight?
The same birds sing? On their great seas
Do ships like ours, with canvas white,
Move stately, answering to the breeze?

Have they their Christ, their Christmas Day?
Know they Mahomet? Buddha? One,
Or all or none? And do they pray?
And have they wrought as we have done?

We cannot guess; 'tis hard indeed,
Our own orb's tale of its dim past
Through centuries untold to read,
And who its future shall forecast?

We only know it keeps its place,
An atom in the universe,
As through the awful realms of space
The mighty hosts of stars disperse.

We know the hand that holds in check
The whirling worlds, each in its course,
And saves the universe from wreck
And peril, this tremendous Force

Holds likewise all our little lives;
The suns and stars do all obey
His bidding, never planet strives
To swerve from its appointed way.

The dangerous boon alone to us
Is given, to choose 'twixt ill and well,
Rebellion or obedience, — thus
To build our heaven, or dig our hell.

But one great thought our strength upholds:
Nothing shall perish! Though his rod
Smites sore, his mercy still enfolds
His own; God's souls are safe with God.

TYRE AND SIDON

Be thou ashamed, Sidon, saith the sea!
The loud voice of the world is in thine ears,
The world thy service hath and ruleth thee,
Thou givest unto vanity thy years.

Hearken, Tyre! For God stretched forth his hand
Over the sea and He the kingdoms shook,
The broad earth quaked at breath of his command,
From thy proud head the gleaming crown He took.

Is this the joyous city wont to boast
Antiquity of ancient days? Behold
Her feet shall carry her afar, her ghost
Shall mourn in desolation and in cold.

Because the promise of Eternal life
And endless glory and unchanging good
Was naught to her, and she chose sin and strife,
Vain mocking shows, and empty husks for food;

Because so eagerly she served the world
Choosing the base and temporal things it gave,
Down from her throne her haughtiness is hurled,
And all her pride is leveled to a grave.

HJELMA

Stands Hjelma at her lady's chair,
Serving with ready hands,
About her head her shining hair
Braided in golden strands.

A rose blooms in her maiden cheek,
And on her mouth's repose
A sweet content she cannot speak
Is lovelier than the rose.

"What is that shrill and sudden cry,
My little maiden? Say!"
"The wild wind shakes the windows high,
And tears the sea to spray;

"Oh see you not the black, black sky,
My mistress dear?" cries she.
"The squall comes down, the waves run high;
Oh hear you not the sea?

"Oh glad am I the boats are in,
And little Nils and Lars
Are safe, before the waves begin

To leap across the stars!"

And up and down and here and there
She goes with willing feet,
So busy, with that gentle air
Of still contentment sweet!

At the far reef, since morning light,
All day her brothers twain
About the wreck of yesternight
Have worked with might and main,

She knows not when the cruel gale
Made wild the waning day,
It seized upon their shivering sail
And flung their skiff away.

She knows not they are driven, lost,
Over the roaring brine,
Toward the dim, billow-beaten coast,
While heaven will make no sign,

But scatters down its freezing snow
To hide the fading light,
And drives its hurricane below
To fright the shuddering night.

She hums her sweet Norwegian songs,
She lights the lamps, and smiles;
The breakers rash in raging throngs
Across the lonely miles.

And where is handsome Lars, so tall?
And where is Nils, so dear?
Upon her soul no shadows fall,
Nor any hint of fear.

And who shall speak to break the spell?
And who will deal the blow?
The brothers twain she loved so well,
Their fate must Hjelma know!

Loud thunders on the savage storm,
With deep, defiant roar;
Unconscious in her shelter warm
She hears it lash the shore.

And brightly shines her braided hair,

And on her mouth's repose
Is sweet content, untouched by care,
And on her cheek the rose.

MY HOLLYHOCK

Ah me, my scarlet hollyhock,
Whose stately head the breezes rock,
How sad, that in one night of frost
Thy radiant beauty shall be lost,
And all thy glory overthrown
Ere half thy ruby buds have blown!
All day across my window low
Thy flowery stalk sways to and fro
Against a background of blue sea.
On the south wind, to visit thee,
Come airy shapes in sumptuous dyes,
Rich golden, black- edged butterflies,
And humming-birds in emerald coats,
With flecks of fire upon their throats,
That in the sunshine whir and glance,
And probe the flowers with slender lance;
And many a drunken, drowsy bee,
Singing his song hilariously.
About the garden fluttering yet,
In amber plumage freaked with jet,
The goldfinches charm all the air
With sweet, sad crying everywhere.
To the dry sunflower stalks they cling,
And on the ripened disks they swing;
With delicate delight they feed
On the rich store of milky seed.

Autumn goes loitering through the land,
A torch of fire within her hand.
Soft sleeps the bloomy haze that broods
O'er distant hills and mellowing woods;
Rustle the cornfields far and near,
And nuts are ripe, and pastures sere,
And lovely odors haunt the breeze,
Borne o'er the sea and through the trees.
Belated beauty, lingering still
So near the edge of winter's chill,
The deadly daggers of the cold
Approach thee, and the year grows old.
Is it because I love thee so

Thou waitest, waving to and fro
Thy flowery spike, to gladden me,
Against the background of blue sea?
I wonder — hast thou not some sense,
Some measure of intelligence
Responding to my joy in thee?
Almost I dream that it may be,
Such subtleties are Nature's, hid
Her most well-trodden paths amid;
Such sympathies along her nerves;
Such sweetness in her fine reserves.
Howe'er it be, I thank the powers
That gave me such enchanted hours
This late October, watching thee
Wave thy bright flowers against the sea.

BENEDICTION

"Oh heaven bless you, heaven keep you, sweet!"
It was God's hand that dropped the healing balm
Upon her head, and clothed in prayerful calm
Her soul as saints are robed from head to feet.

Gone is the beautiful beloved voice
That spake that blessing in the vanished years;
Yet in her grateful memory still she hears
The tender tones that made her heart rejoice.

And ever will, while memory keeps her seat;
And though she dwelt among the nameless dead,
Her dust would thrill beneath the voice that said,
"May heaven bless you, heaven keep you, sweet! "

SONNET

If I do speak your praise, forgive me, Sweet!
Since love demands expression, let me say
How joyfully my heart goes out to greet
Your grace and charm with every changing day:
How sweet your morning kiss, how dear your smile,
And tender touch, and voice that's low and clear,
And with what deep content I yield the while
You draw me to you, near and yet more near,
And show me what pure depths within you lie, —

The powers of good, the gentle steadfastness,
The quiet wisdom and the purpose high,
So strong to love, to lift, to cheer and bless;
While like a robe of loveliness you wear
Your flower-like radiance delicately fair.

ON THE TRAIN

Through the storm, through the wind and the rain
Rushes the clattering train;
Past the hills, across valley and plain,
Through city and hamlet again,
With a rumble and roar we speed on
Till the half of our journey is done.

Close wrapped in my corner I dream,
Watching the raindrops stream
O'er the misty pane, and the gleam
Of the white of the steam,
As they hurry past and are lost,
On the wings of the tempest tossed.

Through the smoke and the din and the blur
Fast, fast I am flying to her!
All the thunder, the rattle and whir,
The noisy discomfort, the stir,
Are nothing to me, for my sense
Is lost in a rapture intense.

And like golden bees through the storm
Sweet memories cluster and swarm;
Sweet thoughts round a maidenly form
That I see by the firelight warm, —
Bright eyes that are watching the clock,
Little ears that are waiting my knock;

And I know how the color will rush
In that beautiful mantling blush
To her cheek, till its delicate flush
Shall rival the rose, as I hush
With a word her heart's tumult divine
And she lays her white hand within mine.

Then thunder, thou clattering train,
And roar through the wind and the rain,
Past the hills, across valley and plain

Devour the long leagues! — till again
In the light of my love's happy eyes
The sun of my life shall arise.

PEACE

Calm of the autumn night,
With the glow of a primrose sky
Drowned in a sea of golden light
From the harvest moon on high!

Against the rose of the sky
Winging their silent way,
Darkly the gulls go floating by
In the glow of the dying day.

Infinite peace and calm
In the breast of the ocean wide,
In the air like delicate balm,
In the faint, sweet lapse of the tide.

With the cricket's pensive sound,
With the breath of the late, last rose,
Comes a sense of joy profound,
And a bliss of deep repose.

What is thy mystic charm,
beautiful autumn night!
Not the sigh of the south wind warm,
Not thy harvest moon's pure light;

Not the calm of the glassy sea,
Reflecting thy stars above;
Nor thy perfumes borne to me
On the balmy air I love:

But the soul of all thou art
Calls to the soul in me,
And speaks to my quiet heart
With the voice of sky and sea.

AS LINNETS SING

Nay, wherefore should I seek thy patient ear

To weary thee with words that naught avail!
This faltering voice will not ring true and clear,
It will but break and fail.

And yet I cannot keep back any part
Of my delight; fain would I give thee all
The music that thou makest in my heart,
As David sang to Saul.

Would bring thee garlands sweet and manifold,
Meek violets full of fragrance, — roses, too,
Dark pansies richly streaked with burning gold,
And lilies bright with dew.

But ah, they grow so pallid 'neath my hand!
So scentless and so colorless and frail —
The music cannot reach where thou dost stand,
It will but break and fail.

Still at their source the notes are true and strong,
And as some linnet sings, whose happy breast,
Filled with the summer's rapture, thrills with song
That will not be suppressed,

Until she cannot choose but strive to blend
Her slender silver thread of wavering sound
With all the nobler voices that ascend,
Though lost it be and drowned, —

So sing I to the sun that fills my sky
With warmth and light and health. So I to thee
Send up my broken music ceaselessly,
Silent I cannot be.

RUTH

A baby girl not two years old
Among the phlox and pansies stands,
And full of flowers as they can hold
Her mother fills her little hands,

And bids her cross to where I stay
Within my garden's fragrant space,
And guides her past the poppies gay
'Mid mazes of the blooming place,

Saying, "Go carry Thea these!"
Delighted, forth the baby fares,
Between the fluttering-winged sweet peas
Her treasured buds she safely bears.

'T is but a step, but oh, what stress
Of care! What difficulties wait!
How many pretty dangers press
Upon the path from gate to gate!

But high above her sunny head
She tries the roses sweet to hold,
Now caught in coreopsis red,
Half wrecked upon a marigold,

Or tangled in a cornflower tall,
Or hindered by the poppy-tops, —
She struggles on, nor does she fall,
Nor stalk nor stem her progress stops,

Until at last, the trials past,
Victorious o'er the path's alarms,
Herself, her flowers and all are cast
Breathless into my happy arms.

My smiling, rosy little maid!
And while her joy -flushed cheek I kiss,
And close to mine its bloom is laid,
I think, " So may you find your bliss,

"My precious! When in coming years
Life's path grows a bewildering maze,
So may you conquer doubts and fears
And safely thread its devious ways,

"And find yourself, all dangers past,
Clasped to a fonder breast than mine,
And gain your heavenly joy at last
Safe in the arms of Love Divine."

PETITION

My little grandson three years old
Sleeps by my bedside nightly,
Through the long hours of dark and cold,
Dreaming he slumbers lightly.

He feels my love around him fold,
And in its heart reposes,
Upon his hair a gleam of gold,
His cheeks like damask roses.

All through the chill and silent night
I stretch a hand caressing
To draw the blanket, warm and light,
About him, with a blessing.

In sleep he knows that touch so sweet,
So lingering and tender,
Turns his dear face my palm to meet,
With soft and glad surrender.

O God of pity and of love,
Have patience with our blindness,
Thy hand is stretched our heads above
Warm with Thy watchful kindness.

Give us this baby's perfect faith!
Whatever ills assail us,
Help us to feel, in life or death,
That Thou wilt never fail us.

APPEAL

The childish voice rose to my ear
Sweet toned and eager, praying me,
"I am so little, Granna dear,
Please lift me up, so I can see."

I looked down at the pleading face,
Felt the small hand's entreating touch,
And stooping caught in swift embrace
The baby boy I loved so much,

And held him high that he might gaze
At the great pageant of the sky,
The glory of the sunset's blaze,
The glittering moon that curved on high.

With speechless love I clasped him close
And read their beauty in his eyes,
And on his fair cheek kissed the rose,

Sweeter than blooms of Paradise.

And in my heart his eager prayer
Found echo, and the self-same cry
Rose from my heart through heaven's air,
"O gracious Father, lift me high!

"So little and so low am I,
Among earth's mists I call to Thee,
Show me the glory of Thy sky!
Oh lift me up that I may see!"

A MEMORABLE MURDER. A TRUE STORY.

At the Isles of Shoals, on the 5th of March in the year 1873, occurred one of the most monstrous tragedies ever enacted on this planet. The sickening details of the double murder are well known; the newspapers teemed with them for months: but the pathos of the story is not realized; the world does not know how gentle a life these poor people led, how innocently happy were their quiet days. They were all Norwegians. The more I see of the natives of this far-off land, the more I admire the fine qualities which seem to characterize them as a race. Gentle, faithful, intelligent, God-fearing human beings, they daily use such courtesy toward each other and all who come in contact with them, as puts our ruder Yankee manners to shame. The men and women living on this lonely island were like the sweet, honest, simple folk we read of in Bjornson's charming Norwegian stories, full of kindly thoughts and ways. The murdered Anethe might have been the Eli of Bjornson's beautiful Arne or the Ragnhild of Boyesen's lovely romance. They rejoiced to find a home just such as they desired in this peaceful place; the women took such pleasure in the little house which they kept so neat and bright, in their flock of hens, their little dog Ringe, and all their humble belongings! The Norwegians are an exceptionally affectionate people; family ties are very strong and precious among them. Let me tell the story of their sorrow as simply as may be.

Louis Wagner murdered Anethe and Karen Christensen at midnight on the 5th of March, two years ago this spring. The whole affair shows the calmness of a practiced hand; there was no malice in the deed, no heat; it was one of the coolest instances of deliberation ever chronicled in the annals of crime. He admits that these people had shown him nothing but kindness. He says in so many words, "They were my best friends." They looked upon him as a brother. Yet he did not hesitate to murder them. The island called Smutty-Nose by human perversity (since in old times it bore the pleasanter title of Haley's Island) was selected to be the scene of this disaster. Long ago I lived two years upon it, and know well its whitened ledges and grassy slopes, its low thickets of wild-rose and bayberry, its sea-wall still intact, connecting it with the small island Malaga, opposite Appledore, and the ruined break-water which links it with Cedar Island on the other side. A lonely cairn, erected by some long ago forgotten fishermen or sailors, stands upon the highest rock at the southeastern extremity; at its western end a few houses are scattered, small, rude dwellings, with the square old Haley house near; two or three fish-houses are falling into decay about the water-side, and the ancient wharf drops stone by stone into the little cove, where every day the tide ebbs and flows and ebbs again with pleasant sound and freshness. Near the houses is a small grave-yard, where a few of the natives sleep, and not far, the graves of the fourteen

Spaniards lost in the wreck of the ship Sagunto in the year 1813. I used to think it was a pleasant place, that low, rocky, and grassy island, though so wild and lonely.

From the little town of Laurvig, near Christiania, in Norway, came John and Maren Hontvet to this country, and five years ago took up their abode in this desolate spot, in one of the cottages facing the cove and Appledore. And there they lived through the long winters and the lovely summers, John making a comfortable living by fishing, Maren, his wife, keeping as bright and tidy and sweet a little home for him as man could desire. The bit of garden they cultivated in the summer was a pleasure to them; they made their house as pretty as they could with paint and paper and gay pictures, and Maren had a shelf for her plants at the window; and John was always so good to her, so kind and thoughtful of her comfort and of what would please her, she was entirely happy. Sometimes she was a little lonely, perhaps, when he was tossing afar off on the sea, setting or hauling his trawls, or had sailed to Portsmouth to sell his fish. So that she was doubly glad when the news came that some of her people were coming over from Norway to live with her. And first, in the month of May, 1871, came her sister Karen, who stayed only a short time with Maren, and then came to Appledore, where she lived at service two years, till within a fortnight of her death. The first time I saw Maren, she brought her sister to us, and I was charmed with the little woman's beautiful behavior; she was so gentle, courteous, decorous, she left on my mind a most delightful impression. Her face struck me as remarkably good and intelligent, and her gray eyes were full of light.

Karen was a rather sad-looking woman, about twenty-nine years old; she had lost a lover in Norway long since, and in her heart she fretted and mourned for this continually: she could not speak a word of English at first, but went patiently about her work and soon learned enough, and proved herself an excellent servant, doing faithfully and thoroughly everything she under took, as is the way of her people generally. Her personal neatness was most attractive. She wore gowns made of cloth woven by herself in Norway, a coarse blue stuff, always neat and clean, and often I used to watch her as she sat by the fire spinning at a spinning-wheel brought from her own country; she made such a pretty picture, with her blue gown and fresh white apron, and the nice, clear white muslin bow with which she was in the habit of fastening her linen collar, that she was very agreeable to look upon. She had a pensive way of letting her head droop a little sideways as she spun, and while the low wheel hummed monotonously, she would sit crooning sweet, sad old Norwegian airs by the hour together, perfectly unconscious that she was affording such pleasure to a pair of appreciative eyes. On the 12th of October, 1872, in the second year of her stay with us, her brother, Ivan Christensen, and his wife, Anethe Mathea, came over from their Norseland in an evil day, and joined Maren and John at their island, living in the same house with them.

Ivan and Anethe had been married only since Christmas of the preceding year. Ivan was tall, light haired, rather quiet and grave. Anethe was young, fair, and merry, with thick, bright sunny hair, which was so long it reached, when unbraided, nearly to her knees; blue-eyed, with brilliant teeth and clear, fresh complexion, beautiful, and beloved beyond expression by her young husband, Ivan. Mathew Hontvet, John's brother, had also joined the little circle a year before, and now Maren's happiness was complete. Delighted to welcome them all, she made all things pleasant for them, and she told me only a few days ago, "I never was so happy in my life as when we were all living there together." So they abode in peace and quiet, with not an evil thought in their minds, kind and considerate toward each other, the men devoted to their women and the women repaying them with interest, till out of the perfectly cloudless sky one day a blot descended, without a whisper of warning, and brought ruin and desolation into that peaceful home.

Louis Wagner, who had been in this country seven years, appeared at the Shoals two years before the date of the murder. He lived about the islands during that time. He was born in Ueckermunde, a small town of lower Pomeranie, in Northern Prussia. Very little is known about him, though there were vague rumors that his past life had not been without difficulties, and he had boasted foolishly among his mates that "not many had done what he had done and got off in safety;" but people did not trouble themselves about him or his past, all having enough to do to earn their bread and keep the wolf from the door. Maren describes him as tall, powerful, dark, with a peculiarly quiet manner. She says she never saw him drunk—he seemed always anxious to keep his wits about him: he would linger on the outskirts of a drunken brawl, listening to and absorbing everything, but never mixing himself up in any disturbance. He was always lurking in corners, lingering, looking, listening, and he would look no man straight in the eyes. She spoke, however, of having once heard him disputing with some sailors, at table, about some point of navigation; she did not understand it, but all were against Louis, and, waxing warm, all strove to show him he was in the wrong. As he rose and left the table she heard him mutter to himself with an oath, "I know I'm wrong, but I'll never give in!" During the winter preceding the one in which his hideous deed was committed, he lived at Star Island and fished alone, in a wherry; but he made very little money, and came often over to the Hontvets, where Maren gave him food when he was suffering from want, and where he received always a welcome and the utmost kindness. In the following June he joined Hontvet in his business of fishing, and took up his abode as one of the family at Smutty-Nose. During the summer he was "crippled," as he said, by the rheumatism, and they were all very good to him, and sheltered, fed, nursed, and waited upon him the greater part of the season. He remained with them five weeks after Ivan and Anethe arrived, so that he grew to know Anethe as well as Maren, and was looked upon as a brother by all of them, as I have said before. Nothing occurred to show his true character, and in November he left the island and the kind people whose hospitality he was to repay so fearfully, and going to Portsmouth he took passage in another fishing schooner, the Addison Gilbert, which was presently wrecked off the coast, and he was again thrown out of employment. Very recklessly he said to Waldemar Ingebertsen, to Charles Jonsen, and even to John Hontvet himself, at different times, that "he must have money if he murdered for it." He loafed about Portsmouth eight weeks, doing nothing. Meanwhile Karen left our service in February, intending to go to Boston and work at a sewing machine, for she was not strong and thought she should like it better than housework, but before going she lingered awhile with her sister Maren-fatal delay for her! Maren told me that during this time Karen went to Portsmouth and had her teeth removed, meaning to provide herself with a new set. At the Jonsens', where Louis was staying, one day she spoke to Mrs. Jonsen of her mouth, that it was so sensitive since the teeth had been taken out; and Mrs. Jonsen asked her how long she must wait before the new set could be put in. Karen replied that it would be three months. Louis Wagner was walking up and down at the other end of the room with his arms folded, his favorite attitude. Mrs. Jonsen's daughter passed near him and heard him mutter, "Three months! What is the use! In three months you will be dead!" He did not know the girl was so near, and turning, he confronted her. He knew she must have heard what he said, and he glared at her like a wild man.

On the fifth day of March, 1873, John Hontvet, his brother Mathew, and Ivan Christensen set sail in John's little schooner, the Clara Bella, to draw their trawls. At that time four of the islands were inhabited: one family on White Island, at the light-house; the workmen who were building the new hotel on Star Island, and one or two households beside; the Hontvet family at Smutty-Nose; and on Appledore, the household at the large house, and on the southern side, opposite Smutty-Nose, a little cottage, where lived Jorge Edvardt Ingebertsen, his wife and children, and several men who fished with him. Smutty-Nose is not in sight of the large house at Appledore, so we were in ignorance of all that happened on that dreadful night, longer than the other inhabitants of the Shoals.

John, Ivan, and Mathew went to draw their trawls, which had been set some miles to the eastward of the islands. They intended to be back to dinner, and then to go on to Portsmouth with their fish, and bait the trawls afresh, ready to bring back to set again next day. But the wind was strong and fair for Portsmouth and ahead for the island; it would have been a long beat home against it; so they went on to Portsmouth, without touching at the island to leave one man to guard the women, as had been their custom. This was the first night in all the years Maren had lived there that the house was without a man to protect it. But John, always thoughtful for her, asked Emil Ingebertsen, whom he met on the fishing-grounds, to go over from Appledore and tell her that they had gone on to Portsmouth with the favoring wind, but that they hoped to be back that night. And he would have been back had the bait he expected from Boston arrived on the train in which it was due. How curiously everything adjusted itself to favor the bringing about of this horrible catastrophe! The bait did not arrive till the half past twelve train, and they were obliged to work the whole night getting their trawls ready, thus leaving the way perfectly clear for Louis Wagner's awful work.

The three women left alone watched and waited in vain for the schooner to return, and kept the dinner hot for the men, and patiently wondered why they did not come. In vain they searched the wide horizon for that returning sail. Ah me, what pathos is in that longing look of women's eyes for far off sails! that gaze so eager, so steadfast, that it would almost seem as if it must conjure up the ghostly shape of glimmering canvas from the mysterious distances of sea and sky, and draw it unerringly home by the mere force of intense wistfulness! And those gentle eyes, that were never to see the light of another sun, looked anxiously across the heaving sea till twilight fell, and then John's messenger, Emil, arrived —Emil Ingebertsen, courteous and gentle as a youthful knight—and reassured them with his explanation, which having given, he departed, leaving them in a much more cheerful state of mind. So the three sisters, with only the little dog Ringe for a protector, sat by the fire chatting together cheerfully. They fully expected the schooner back again that night from Portsmouth, but they were not ill at ease while they waited. Of what should they be afraid? They had not an enemy in the world! No shadow crept to the fireside to warn them what was at hand, no portent of death chilled the air as they talked their pleasant talk and made their little plans in utter unconsciousness. Karen was to have gone to Portsmouth with the fishermen that day; she was all ready dressed to go. Various little commissions were given her, errands to do for the two sisters she was to leave behind. Maren wanted some buttons, and "I'll give you one for a pattern; I'll put it in your purse," she said to Karen, "and then when you open your purse you'll be sure to remember it." (That little button, of a peculiar pattern, was found in Wagner's possession afterward.) They sat up till ten o'clock, talking together. The night was bright and calm; it was a comfort to miss the bitter winds that had raved about the little dwelling all the long, rough winter. Already it was spring; this calm was the first token of its coming. It was the 6th of March; in a few weeks the weather would soften, the grass grow green, and Anethe would see the first flowers in this strange country, so far from her home where she had left father and mother, kith and kin, for love of Ivan. The delicious days of summer at hand would transform the work of the toiling fishermen to pleasure, and all things would bloom and smile about the poor people on the lonely rock! Alas, it was not to be.

At ten o'clock they went to bed. It was cold and "lonesome" up-stairs, so Maren put some chairs by the side of the lounge, laid a mattress upon it, and made up a bed for Karen in the kitchen, where she presently fell asleep. Maren and Anethe slept in the next room. So safe they felt themselves, they did not pull down a curtain, nor even try to fasten the house-door. They went to their rest in absolute security and perfect trust. It was the first still night of the new year; a young moon stole softly down toward the west, a gentle wind breathed through the quiet dark, and the waves whispered gently about the island, helping to lull those innocent souls to yet more peaceful slumber. Ah, where were the gales of March that night have plowed that tranquil sea to foam, and cut off the fatal path of Louis Wagner to that happy home! But nature seemed to pause and wait for him. I remember looking abroad over the waves that night and rejoicing over "the first calm night of the year!" It was so still, so bright! The hope of all the light and beauty a few weeks would bring forth stirred me to sudden joy. There should be spring again after the long winter weariness.

"Can trouble live in April days,
Or sadness in the summer moons?"

I thought, as I watched the clear sky, grown less hard than it had been for weeks, and sparkling with stars. But before another sunset it seemed to me that beauty had fled out of the world, and that goodness, innocence, mercy, gentleness, were a mere mockery of empty words.

Here let us leave the poor women, asleep on the lonely rock, with no help near them in heaven or upon earth, and follow the fishermen to Portsmouth, where they arrived about four o'clock that afternoon. One of the first men whom they saw as they neared the town was Louis Wagner; to him they threw the rope from the schooner, and he helped draw her in to the wharf. Greetings passed between them; he spoke to Mathew Hontvet, and as he looked at Ivan Christensen, the men noticed a flush pass over Louis's face. He asked were they going out again that night? Three times before they parted he asked that question; he saw that all the three men belonging to the island had come away together; he began to realize his opportunity. They answered him that if their bait came by the train in which they expected it, they hoped to get back that night, but if it was late they should be obliged to stay till morning, baiting their trawls; and they asked him to come and help them. It is a long and tedious business, the baiting of trawls; often more than a thousand hooks are to be manipulated, and lines and hooks coiled, clear of tangles, into tubs, all ready for throwing overboard when the fishing-grounds are reached. Louis gave them a half promise that he would help them, but they did not see him again after leaving the wharf. The three fishermen were hungry, not having touched at their island, where Maren always provided them with a supply of food to take with them; they asked each other if either had brought any money with which to buy bread, and it came out that every one had left his pocketbook at home. Louis, standing by, heard all this. He asked John, then, if he had made fishing pay. John answered that he had cleared about six hundred dollars.

The men parted, the honest three about their business; but Louis, what became of him with his evil thoughts? At about half past seven he went into a liquor shop and had a glass of something; not enough to make him unsteady,—he was too wise for that. He was not seen again in Portsmouth by any human creature that night. He must have gone, after that, directly down to the river, that beautiful, broad river, the Piscataqua, upon whose southern bank the quaint old city of Portsmouth dreams its quiet days away; and there he found a boat ready to his hand, a dory belonging to a man by the name of David Burke, who had that day furnished it with new thole-pins. When it was picked up afterward off the mouth of the river, Louis's anxious oars had eaten half-way through the substance of these pins, which are always made of the hardest, toughest wood that can be found. A terrible piece of rowing must that have been, in one night! Twelve miles from the city to the Shoals,— three to the light-houses, where the river meets the open sea, nine more to the islands; nine back again to Newcastle next morning! He took that boat, and with the favoring tide dropped down the rapid river where the swift current is so strong that oars are scarcely needed, except to keep the boat steady. Truly all nature seemed to play into his hands; this first relenting night of earliest spring favored him with its stillness, the tide was fair, the wind was fair, the little moon gave him just enough light, without betraying him to any curious eyes, as he glided down the three miles between the river banks, in haste to reach the sea. Doubtless the light west wind played about him as delicately as if he had been the most human of God's creatures; nothing breathed remonstrance in his ear, nothing whispered in the whispering water that rippled about his inexorable keel, steering straight for the Shoals through the quiet darkness. The snow lay thick and white upon the land in the moonlight; lamps twinkled here and there from dwellings on either side; in Eliot and Newcastle, in Portsmouth and Kittery, roofs, chimneys, and gables showed faintly in the vague light; the leafless trees clustered dark in hollows or lifted their tracery of bare boughs in higher spaces against the wintry sky. His eyes must have looked on it all, whether he saw the peaceful picture or not. Beneath many a humble roof honest folk were settling into their untroubled rest, as "this planned piece of deliberate wickedness" was stealing silently by with his heart full of darkness, blacker than the black tide that swirled beneath his boat and bore him fiercely on. At the river's mouth stood the sentinel light-houses, sending their great spokes of light afar into the night, like the arms of a wide humanity stretching into the darkness helping hands to bring all who needed succor safely home. He passed them, first the tower at Fort Point, then the taller one at Whale's Back, steadfastly holding aloft their warning fires. There was no signal from the warning bell as he rowed by, though a danger more subtle, more deadly, than fog, or hurricane, or pelting storm was passing swift beneath it. Unchallenged by anything in earth or heaven, he kept on his way and gained the great outer ocean, doubtless pulling strong and steadily, for he had no time to lose, and the longest night was all too short for an under taking such as this. Nine miles from the light-houses to the islands! Slowly he makes his way; it seems to take an eternity of time. And now he is midway between the islands and the coast. That little toy of a boat with its one occupant in the midst of the awful, black, heaving sea! The vast dim ocean whispers with a thousand waves; against the boat's side the ripples lightly tap, and pass and are lost; the air is full of fine, mysterious voices of winds and waters. Has he no fear, alone there on the midnight sea with such a purpose in his heart? The moonlight sends a long, golden track across the waves; it touches his dark face and figure, it glitters on his dripping oars. On his right hand Boone Island light shows like a setting star on the horizon, low on his left the two beacons twinkle off Newburyport, at the mouth of the Merrimack River; all the light-houses stand watching along the coast, wheeling their long, slender shafts of radiance as if pointing at this black atom creeping over the face of the planet with such colossal evil in his heart. Before him glitters the Shoals' light at White Island, and helps to guide him to his prey. Alas, my friendly light house, that you should serve so terrible a purpose! Steadily the oars click in the rowlocks; stroke after stroke of the broad blades draws him away from the lessening line of land, over the wavering floor of the ocean, nearer the lonely rocks. Slowly the coast-lights fade, and now the rote of the sea among the lonely ledges of the Shoals salutes his attentive ear. A little longer and he nears Appledore, the first island, and now he passes by the snow-covered, ice-bound rock, with the long buildings showing clear in the moonlight. He must have looked at them as he went past. I wonder we who slept beneath the roofs that glimmered to his eyes in the uncertain light did not feel, through the thick veil of sleep, what fearful thing passed by! But we slumbered peacefully as the unhappy women whose doom every click of those oars in the rowlocks, like the ticking of some dreadful clock, was bringing nearer and nearer. Between the islands he passes; they are full of chilly gleams and glooms. There is no scene more weird than these snow-covered rocks in winter, more shudderful and strange: the moonlight touching them with mystic glimmer, the black water breaking about them and the vast shadowy spaces of the sea stretching to the horizon on every side, full of vague sounds, of half lights and shadows, of fear, and of mystery. The island he seeks lies before him, lone and still; there is no gleam in any window, there is no help near, nothing upon which the women can call for succor. He does not land in the cove where all boats put in, he rows round to the south side and draws his boat up on the rocks. His red returning footsteps are found here next day, staining the snow. He makes his way to the house he knows so well.

All is silent: nothing moves, nothing sounds but the hushed voices of the sea. His hand is on the latch, he enters stealthily, there is nothing to resist him. The little dog, Ringe, begins to bark sharp and loud, and

Karen rouses, crying, "John, is that you?" thinking the expected fishermen had returned. Louis seizes a chair and strikes at her in the dark; the clock on a shelf above her head falls down with the jarring of the blow, and stops at exactly seven minutes to one. Maren in the next room, waked suddenly from her sound sleep, trying in vain to make out the meaning of it all, cries, "What's the matter?" Karen answers, "John scared me!" Maren springs from her bed and tries to open her chamber door; Louis has fastened it on the other side by pushing a stick through the latch. With her heart leaping with terror the poor child shakes the door with all her might, in vain. Utterly confounded and bewildered, she hears Karen screaming, "John kills me! John kills me!" She hears the sound of repeated blows and shrieks, till at last her sister falls heavily against the door, which gives way, and Maren rushes out. She catches dimly a glimpse of a tall figure outlined against the southern window; she seizes poor Karen and drags her with the strength of frenzy within the bedroom. This unknown terror, this fierce, dumb monster who never utters a sound to betray himself through the whole, pursues her with blows, strikes her three times with a chair, either blow with fury sufficient to kill her, had it been light enough for him to see how to direct it; but she gets her sister inside and the door shut, and holds it against him with all her might and Karen's failing strength. What a little heroine was this poor child, struggling with the force of desperation to save herself and her sisters!

All this time Anethe lay dumb, not daring to move or breathe, roused from the deep sleep of youth and health by this nameless, formless terror. Maren, while she strives to hold the door at which Louis rattles again and again, calls to her in anguish, "Anethe, Anethe! Get out of the window! run! hide!" The poor girl, almost paralyzed with fear, tries to obey, puts her bare feet out of the low window, and stands outside in the freezing snow, with one light garment over her cowering figure, shrinking in the cold winter wind, the clear moonlight touching her white face and bright hair and fair young shoulders. "Scream! scream!" shouts frantic Maren. "Somebody at Star Island may hear!" but Anethe answers with the calmness of despair, "I cannot make a sound." Maren screams, herself, but the feeble sound avails nothing. "Run! run!" she cries to Anethe; but again Anethe answers, "I cannot move."

Louis has left off trying to force the door; he listens. Are the women trying to escape? He goes out of doors. Maren flies to the window; he comes round the corner of the house and confronts Anethe where she stands in the snow. The moonlight shines full in his face; she shrieks loudly and distinctly, "Louis, Louis!" Ah, he is discovered, he is recognized! Quick as thought he goes back to the front door, at the side of which stands an ax, left there by Maren, who had used it the day before to cut the ice from the well. He returns to Anethe standing shuddering there. It is no matter that she is beautiful, young, and helpless to resist, that she has been kind to him, that she never did a human creature harm, that she stretches her gentle hands out to him in agonized entreaty, crying piteously, "Oh, Louis, Louis, Louis!" He raises the ax and brings it down on her bright head in one tremendous blow, and she sinks without a sound and lies in a heap, with her warm blood reddening the snow. Then he deals her blow after blow, almost within reach of Maren's hands, as she stands at the window. Distracted, Maren strives to rouse poor Karen, who kneels with her head on the side of the bed; with desperate entreaty she tries to get her up and away, but Karen moans, "I cannot, I cannot." She is too far gone; and then Maren knows she cannot save her, and that she must flee herself or die. So, while Louis again enters the house, she seizes a skirt and wraps round her shoulders, and makes her way out of the open window, over Anethe's murdered body, barefooted, flying away, anywhere, breathless, shaking with terror.

Where can she go? Her little dog, frightened into silence, follows her,—pressing so close to her feet that she falls over him more than once. Looking back she sees Louis has lit a lamp and is seeking for her. She flies to the cove; if she can but find his boat and row away in it and get help! It is not there; there is no boat in which she can get away. She hears Karen's wild screams, he is killing her! Oh where can she go?

Is there any place on that little island where he will not find her? She thinks she will creep into one of the empty old houses by the water; but no, she reflects, if I hide there, Ringe will bark and betray me the moment Louis comes to look for me. And Ringe saved her life, for next day Louis's bloody tracks were found all about those old buildings where he had sought her. She flies, with Karen's awful cries in her ears, away over rocks and snow to the farthest limit she can gain. The moon has set; it is about two o'clock in the morning, and oh, so cold! She shivers and shudders from head to feet, but her agony of terror is so great she is hardly conscious of bodily sensation. And welcome is the freezing snow, the jagged ice and iron rocks that tear her unprotected feet, the bitter brine that beats against the shore, the winter winds that make her shrink and tremble; "they are not so unkind as man's ingratitude!" Falling often, rising, struggling on with feverish haste, she makes her way to the very edge of the water; down almost into the sea she creeps, between two rocks, upon her hands and knees, and crouches, face downward, with Ringe nestled close beneath her breast, not daring to move through the long hours that must pass before the sun will rise again. She is so near the ocean she can almost reach the water with her hand. Had the wind breathed the least roughly the waves must have washed over her. There let us leave her and go back to Louis Wagner. Maren heard her sister Karen's shrieks as she fled. The poor girl had crept into an unoccupied room in a distant part of the house, striving to hide herself. He could not kill her with blows, blundering in the darkness, so he wound a handkerchief about her throat and strangled her. But now he seeks anxiously for Maren. Has she escaped? What terror is in the thought! Escaped, to tell the tale, to accuse him as the murderer of her sisters. Hurriedly, with desperate anxiety, he seeks for her. His time was growing short; it was not in his programme that this brave little creature should give him so much trouble; he had not calculated on resistance from these weak and helpless women. Already it was morning, soon it would be daylight. He could not find her in or near the house; he went down to the empty and dilapidated houses about the cove, and sought her everywhere. What a picture! That blood-stained butcher, with his dark face, crawling about those cellars, peering for that woman! He dared not spend any more time; he must go back for the money he hoped to find, his reward for this! All about the house he searches, in bureau drawers, in trunks and boxes: he finds fifteen dollars for his night's work! Several hundreds were lying between some sheets folded at the bottom of a drawer in which he looked. But he cannot stop for more thorough investigation; a dreadful haste pursues him like a thousand fiends. He drags Anethe's stiffening body into the house, and leaves it on the kitchen floor. If the thought crosses his mind to set fire to the house and burn up his two victims, he dares not do it: it will make a fatal bon fire to light his homeward way; besides, it is useless, for Maren has escaped to accuse him, and the time presses so horribly! But how cool a monster is he! After all this hard work he must have refreshment to support him in the long row back to the land; knife and fork, cup and plate, were found next morning on the table near where Anethe lay; fragments of food which was not cooked in the house, but brought from Portsmouth, were scattered about. Tidy Maren had left neither dishes nor food when they went to bed. The handle of the tea-pot which she had left on the stove was stained and smeared with blood. Can the human mind conceive of such hideous nonchalance? Wagner sat down in that room and ate and drank! It is almost beyond belief! Then he went to the well with a basin and towels, tried to wash off the blood, and left towels and basin in the well. He knows he must be gone! It is certain death to linger. He takes his boat and rows away toward the dark coast and the twinkling lights; it is for dear life, now! What powerful strokes send the small skiff rushing over the water!

There is no longer any moon, the night is far spent; already the east changes, the stars fade; he rows like a madman to reach the land, but a blush of morning is stealing up the sky and sunrise is rosy over shore and sea, when panting, trembling, weary, a creature accursed, a blot on the face of the day, he lands at Newcastle—too late! Too late! In vain he casts the dory adrift; she will not float away; the flood tide bears her back to give her testimony against him, and afterward she is found at Jaffrey's Point, near the

"Devil's Den," and the fact of her worn thole-pins noted. Wet, covered with ice from the spray which has flown from his eager oars, utterly exhausted, he creeps to a knoll and reconnoitres; he thinks he is unobserved, and crawls on towards Portsmouth. But he is seen and recognized by many persons, and his identity established beyond a doubt. He goes to the house of Mathew Jonsen, where he has been living, steals up-stairs, changes his clothes, and appears before the family, anxious, frightened, agitated, telling Jonsen he never felt so badly in his life; that he has got into trouble and is afraid he shall be taken. He cannot eat at breakfast, says "farewell forever," goes away and is shaved, and takes the train to Boston, where he provides himself with new clothes, shoes, a complete outfit, but lingering, held by fate, he cannot fly, and before night the officer's hand is on his shoulder and he is arrested.

Meanwhile poor shuddering Maren on the lonely island, by the water-side, waits till the sun is high in heaven before she dares come forth. She thinks he may be still on the island. She said to me, "I thought he must be there, dead or alive. I thought he might go crazy and kill himself after having done all that." At last she steals out. The little dog frisks before her; it is so cold her feet cling to the rocks and snow at every step, till the skin is fairly torn off. Still and frosty is the bright morning, the water lies smiling and sparkling, the hammers of the workmen building the new hotel on Star Island sound through the quiet air. Being on the side of Smutty-Nose opposite Star, she waves her skirt, and screams to attract their attention; they hear her, turn and look, see a woman waving a signal of distress, and, surprising to relate, turn tranquilly to their work again. She realizes at last there is no hope in that direction; she must go round toward Appledore in sight of the dreadful house. Passing it afar off she gives one swift glance toward it, terrified lest in the broad sunshine she may see some horrid token of last night's work; but all is still and peaceful. She notices the curtains the three had left up when they went to bed; they are now drawn down; she knows whose hand has done this, and what it hides from the light of day. Sick at heart, she makes her painful way to the northern edge of Malaga, which is connected with Smutty-Nose by the old sea-wall. She is directly opposite Appledore and the little cottage where abide her friend and countryman, Jorge Edvardt Ingebertsen, and his wife and children. Only a quarter of a mile of the still ocean separates her from safety and comfort. She sees the children playing about the door; she calls and calls. Will no one ever hear her? Her torn feet torment her, she is sore with blows and perishing with cold. At last her voice reaches the ears of the children, who run and tell their father that some one is crying and calling; looking across, he sees the poor little figure waving her arms, takes his dory and paddles over, and with amazement recognizes Maren in her night-dress, with bare feet and streaming hair, with a cruel bruise upon her face, with wild eyes, distracted, half senseless with cold and terror. He cries, "Maren, Maren, who has done this? what is it? who is it?" and her only answer is "Louis, Louis, Louis!" as he takes her on board his boat and rows home with her as fast as he can. From her incoherent statement he learns what has happened. Leaving her in the care of his family, he comes over across the hill to the great house on Appledore. As I sit at my desk I see him pass the window, and wonder why the old man comes so fast and anxiously through the heavy snow.

Presently I see him going back again, accompanied by several of his own countrymen and others of our workmen, carrying guns. They are going to Smutty-Nose, and take arms, thinking it possible Wagner may yet be there. I call down-stairs, "What has happened?" and am answered, "Some trouble at Smutty-Nose; we hardly understand." "Probably a drunken brawl of the reckless fishermen who may have landed there," I say to myself, and go on with my work. In another half-hour I see the men returning, reinforced by others, coming fast, confusedly; and suddenly a wail of anguish comes up from the women below. I cannot believe it when I hear them crying, "Karen is dead! Anethe is dead! Louis Wagner has murdered them both!" I run out into the servants' quarters; there are all the men assembled, an awe-stricken crowd. Old Ingebertsen comes forward and tells me the bare facts and how Maren lies at his house, half crazy, suffering with her torn and frozen feet. Then the men are dispatched to search

Appledore, to find if by any chance the murderer might be concealed about the place, and I go over to Maren to see if I can do anything for her. I find the women and children with frightened faces at the little cottage; as I go into the room where Maren lies, she catches my hands, crying, "Oh, I so glad to see you! I so glad I save my life!" and with her dry lips she tells me all the story as I have told it here. Poor little creature, holding me with those wild, glittering', dilated eyes, she cannot tell me rapidly enough the whole horrible tale. Upon her cheek is yet the blood-stain from the blow he struck her with a chair, and she shows me two more upon her shoulder, and her torn feet. I go back for arnica with which to bathe them. What a mockery seems to me the "jocund day" as I emerge into the sun shine, and looking across the space of blue, sparkling water, see the house wherein all that horror lies!

Oh brightly shines the morning sun and glitters on the white sails of the little vessel that comes dancing back from Portsmouth before the favoring wind, with the two husbands on board! How glad they are for the sweet morning and the fair wind that brings them home again! And Ivan sees in fancy Anethe's face all beautiful with welcoming smiles, and John knows how happy his good and faithful Maren will be to see him back again. Alas, how little they dream what lies before them! From Appledore they are signaled to come ashore, and Ivan and Mathew, landing, hear a confused rumor of trouble from tongues that hardly can frame the words that must tell the dreadful truth. Ivan only understands that something is wrong. His one thought is for Anethe; he flies to Ingebertsen's cottage, she may be there; he rushes in like a maniac, crying, "Anethe, Anethe! Where is Anethe?" and broken-hearted Maren answers her brother, "Anethe is—at home." He does not wait for another word, but seizes the little boat and lands at the same time with John on Smutty-Nose; with headlong haste they reach the house, other men accompanying them; ah, there are blood-stains all about the snow! Ivan is the first to burst open the door and enter. What words can tell it! There upon the floor, naked, stiff, and stark, is the woman he idolizes, for whose dear feet he could not make life's ways smooth and pleasant enough—stone dead! Dead—horribly butchered! her bright hair stiff with blood, the fair head that had so often rested on his breast crushed! cloven, mangled with the brutal ax! Their eyes are blasted by the intolerable sight: both John and Ivan stagger out and fall, senseless, in the snow. Poor Ivan! his wife a thousand times adored, the dear girl he had brought from Norway, the good, sweet; girl who loved him so, whom he could not cherish tenderly enough! And he was not there to protect her! There was no one there to save her!

"Did Heaven look on
And would not take their part!"

Poor fellow, what had he done that fate should deal him such a blow as this! Dumb, blind with anguish, he made no sign.

"What says the body when they spring
Some monstrous torture engine's whole
Strength on it? No more says the soul."

Some of his pitying comrades lead him away, like one stupefied, and take him back to Appledore. John knows his wife is safe. Though stricken with horror and consumed with wrath, he is not paralyzed like poor Ivan, who has been smitten with worse than death. They find Karen's body in another part of the house, covered with blows and black in the face, strangled. They find Louis's tracks,—all the tokens of his disastrous presence,—the contents of trunks and drawers scattered about in his hasty search for the money, and, all within the house and without, blood, blood everywhere.

When I reach the cottage with the arnica for Maren, they have returned from Smutty-Nose. John, her husband, is there. He is a young man of the true Norse type, blue eyed, fair-haired, tall and well-made, with handsome teeth and bronzed beard. Perhaps he is a little quiet and undemonstrative generally, but at this moment he is superb, kindled from head to feet, a fire-brand of woe and wrath, with eyes that flash and cheeks that burn. I speak a few words to him,—what words can meet such an occasion as this! — and having given directions about the use of the arnica, for Maren, I go away, for nothing more can be done for her, and every comfort she needs is hers. The outer room is full of men; they make way for me, and as I pass through I catch a glimpse of Ivan crouched with his arms thrown round his knees and his head bowed down between them, motionless, his attitude expressing such abandonment of despair as cannot be described. His whole person seems to shrink, as if deprecating the blow that has fallen upon him.

All day the slaughtered women lie as they were found, for nothing can be touched till the officers of the law have seen the whole. And John goes back to Portsmouth to tell his tale to the proper authorities. What a different voyage from the one he had just taken, when happy and careless he was returning to the home he had left so full of peace and comfort! What a load he bears back with him, as he makes his tedious way across the miles that separate him from the means of vengeance he burns to reach! But at last he arrives, tells his story, the police at other cities are at once telegraphed, and the city marshal follows Wagner to Boston. At eight o'clock that evening comes the steamer Mayflower to the Shoals, with all the officers on board. They land and make investigations at Smutty-Nose, then come here to Appledore and examine Maren, and, when everything is done, steam back to Portsmouth, which they reach at three o'clock in the morning. After all are gone and his awful day's work is finished at last, poor John comes back to Maren, and kneeling by the side of her bed, he is utterly overpowered with what he has passed through; he is shaken with sobs as he cries, "Oh, Maren, Maren, it is too much, too much! I cannot bear it!" And Maren throws her arms about his neck, crying, "Oh, John, John, don't! I shall be crazy, I shall die, if you go on like that." Poor innocent, unhappy people, who never wronged a fellow-creature in their lives!

But Ivan—what is their anguish to his! They dare not leave him alone lest he do himself an injury. He is perfectly mute and listless; he cannot weep, he can neither eat nor sleep. He sits like one in a horrid dream. "Oh, my poor, poor brother!" Maren cries in tones of deepest grief, when I speak his name to her next day. She herself cannot rest a moment till she hears that Louis is taken; at every sound her crazed imagination fancies he is coming back for her; she is fairly beside herself with terror and anxiety; but the night following that of the catastrophe brings us news that he is arrested, and there is stern rejoicing at the Shoals; but no vengeance taken on him can bring back those un-offending lives, or restore that gentle home. The dead are properly cared for; the blood is washed from Anethe's beautiful bright hair; she is clothed in her wedding-dress, the blue dress in which she was married, poor child, that happy Christmas time in Norway, a little more than a year ago. They are carried across the sea to Portsmouth, the burial service is read over them, and they are hidden in the earth. After poor Ivan has seen the faces of his wife and sister still and pale in their coffins, their ghastly wounds concealed as much as possible, flowers upon them and the priest praying over them, his trance of misery is broken, the grasp of despair is loosened a little about his heart. Yet hardly does he notice whether the sun shines or no, or care whether he lives or dies. Slowly his senses steady themselves from the effects of a shock that nearly destroyed him, and merciful time, with imperceptible touch, softens day by day the outlines of that picture at the memory of which he will never cease to shudder while he lives.

Louis Wagner was captured in Boston on the evening of the next day after his atrocious deed, and Friday morning, followed by a hooting mob, he was taken to the Eastern depot. At every station along the route crowds were assembled, and there were fierce cries for vengeance. At the depot in Portsmouth a dense crowd of thousands of both sexes had gathered, who assailed him with yells and curses and cries of "Tear him to pieces!" It was with difficulty he was at last safely imprisoned. Poor Maren was taken to Portsmouth from Appledore on that day. The story of Wagner's day in Boston, like every other detail of the affair, has been told by every newspaper in the country: his agitation and restlessness, noted by all who saw him; his curious, reckless talk. To one he says, "I have just killed two sailors;" to another, Jacob Toldtman, into whose shop he goes to buy shoes, "I have seen a woman lie as still as that boot," and so on. When he is caught he puts on a bold face and determines to brave it out; denies everything with tears and virtuous indignation. The men whom he has so fearfully wronged are confronted with him; his attitude is one of injured innocence; he surveys them more in sorrow than in anger, while John is on fire with wrath and indignation, and hurls maledictions at him; but Ivan, poor Ivan, hurt beyond all hope or help, is utterly mute; he does not utter one word. Of what use is it to curse the murderer of his wife? It will not bring her back; he has no heart for cursing, he is too completely broken. Maren told me the first time she was brought into Louis's presence, her heart leaped so fast she could hardly breathe. She entered the room softly with her husband and Mathew Jonsen's daughter. Louis was whittling a stick. He looked up and saw her face, and the color ebbed out of his, and rushed back and stood in one burning spot in his cheek, as he looked at her and she looked at him for a space, in silence. Then he drew about his evil mind the detestable garment of sanctimoniousness, and in sentimental accents he murmured, "I'm glad Jesus loves me!" "The devil loves you!" cried John, with uncompromising veracity. "I know it wasn't nice," said decorous Maren, "but John couldn't help it; it was too much to bear!"

The next Saturday afternoon, when he was to be taken to Saco, hundreds of fishermen came to Portsmouth from all parts of the coast, determined on his destruction, and there was a fearful scene in the quiet streets of that peaceful city when he was being escorted to the train by the police and various officers of justice. Two thousand people had assembled, and such a furious, yelling crowd was never seen or heard in Portsmouth. The air was rent with cries for vengeance; showers of bricks and stones were thrown from all directions, and wounded several of the officers who surrounded Wagner. His knees trembled under him, he shook like an aspen, and the officers found it necessary to drag him along, telling him he must keep up if he would save his life. Except that they feared to injure the innocent as well as the guilty, those men would have literally torn him to pieces. But at last he was put on board the cars in safety, and carried away to prison. His demeanor throughout the term of his confinement, and during his trial and subsequent imprisonment, was a wonderful piece of acting. He really inspired people with doubt as to his guilt. I make an extract from The Portsmouth Chronicle, dated March 13, 1873: "Wagner still retains his amazing sang froid, which is wonderful, even in a strong-nerved German. The sympathy of most of the visitors at his jail has certainly been won by his calmness and his general appearance, which is quite prepossessing." This little instance of his method of proceeding I must subjoin: A lady who had come to converse with him on the subject of his eternal salvation said, as she left him, "I hope you put your trust in the Lord," to which he sweetly answered, "I always did, ma'am, and I always shall."

A few weeks after all this had happened, I sat by the window one afternoon, and, looking up from my work, I saw some one passing slowly,—a young man who seemed so thin, so pale, so bent and ill, that I said, "Here is some stranger who is so very sick, he is probably come to try the effect of the air, even thus early." It was Ivan Christensen. I did not recognize him. He dragged one foot after the other wearily, and walked with the feeble motion of an old man. He entered the house; his errand was to ask for work. He could not bear to go away from the neighborhood of the place where Anethe had lived and where they had been so happy, and he could not bear to work at fishing on the south side of the island, within sight of that house. There was work enough for him here; a kind voice told him so, a kind hand was laid on his shoulder, and he was bidden come and welcome. The tears rushed into the poor fellow's eyes, he went hastily away, and that night sent over his chest of tools,—he was a carpenter by trade. Next day he took up his abode here and worked all summer. Every day I carefully observed him as I passed him by, regarding him with an inexpressible pity, of which he was perfectly unconscious, as he seemed to be of everything and everybody. He never raised his head when he answered my "Good morning," or "Good evening, Ivan." Though I often wished to speak, I never said more to him, for he seemed to me to be hurt too sorely to be touched by human hand. With his head sunk on his breast, and wearily dragging his limbs, he pushed the plane or drove the saw to and fro with a kind of dogged persistence, looking neither to the left nor right. Well might the weight of woe he carried bow him to the earth! By and by he spoke, himself, to other members of the household, saying, with a patient sorrow, he believed it was to have been, it had been so ordered, else why did all things so play into Louis's hands? All things were furnished him: the knowledge of the unprotected state of the women, a perfectly clear field in which to carry out his plans, just the right boat he wanted in which to make his voyage, fair tide, fair wind, calm sea, just moonlight enough; even the ax with which to kill Anethe stood ready to his hand at the house door. Alas, it was to have been! Last summer Ivan went back again to Norway—alone. Hardly is it probable that he will ever return to a land whose welcome to him fate made so horrible. His sister Maren and her husband still live blameless lives, with the little dog Ringe, in a new home they have made for themselves in Portsmouth, not far from the river side; the merciful lapse of days and years takes them gently but surely away from the thought of that season of anguish; and though they can never forget it all, they have grown resigned and quiet again. And on the island other Norwegians have settled, voices of charming children sound sweetly in the solitude that echoed so awfully to the shrieks of Karen and Maren. But to the weirdness of the winter midnight something is added, a vision of two dim, reproachful shades who watch while an agonized ghost prowls eternally about the dilapidated houses at the beach's edge, close by the black, whispering water, seeking for the woman who has escaped him—escaped to bring upon him the death he deserves, whom he never, never, never can find, though his distracted spirit may search till man shall vanish from off the face of the earth, and time shall be no more.

www.ingramcontent.com/pod-product-compliance
Lightning Source LLC
Chambersburg PA
CBHW060134050426
42448CB00010B/2117